ALBERT PUJOLS
SIMPLY THE BEST

Rob Rains

TRIUMPH
BOOKS

Pujols bats in the sixth inning against the San Diego Padres on August 15, 2009. Pujols went 1-for-4 with an RBI and a run scored to extend his hitting streak to 10 games.

This book is available in quantity at special discounts for your group or organization. For further information, contact:
Triumph Books
542 South Dearborn Street
Suite 750
Chicago, Illinois 60605
(312) 939-3330
Fax (312) 663-3557
www.triumphbooks.com

Printed in U.S.A.
ISBN: 978-1-60078-351-7

Design and page production by Mojo Media Inc.
Joe Funk: Editor
Jason Hinman: Creative Director

Photos courtesy of AP Images except where otherwise noted

contents

Foreword

When I was broadcasting the games of the Chicago White Sox, from 1988 through 2005, I always thought I had seen one of the best right-handed hitters ever in Frank Thomas. Then I came to St. Louis in 2006 and saw Albert Pujols.

Albert surpasses Thomas—a two-time Most Valuable Player in the American League. Thomas was a very good hitter—but Albert is a great hitter. Even when he makes an out, he hits the ball hard, and he hits the ball to all fields. He reads pitchers as well as anybody. He picks up on what they throw, what they are tipping off, probably better than anybody. He can take a look at video and read pitchers like a book, and he seems to study everything in the game.

I asked him once, "Where did you learn to play baseball?" He said he learned from his father to be aggressive and to take chances and make things happen. He said he learns every day by watching other players and the way they go about things, and then he puts it into his game.

Albert and Derek Jeter are probably the smartest players in the game. They just seem to take it a step above what you expect. They show up in places on the field where you don't expect them to be.

Albert is a leader, and he just seems to elevate guys around him and make them better. I don't care if it is on the field or off. All the great ones have that aura and personality. When I first met Carlton Fisk, I knew from the way he carried himself that he was a certain Hall of Famer. Being around people in St. Louis like Hall of Famers Stan Musial, Red Schoendienst, Bob Gibson, Lou Brock, Ozzie Smith, and others elsewhere like Johnny Bench, they just have an aura about them. All the great ones do. Albert has that. Albert carries it further because he understands the responsibilities of his position as well as any superstar I've ever been around.

What he does with his foundation is very special. What he does in the Dominican Republic, helping so many people who don't have proper medical or dental care, is really important to him. He's a very sincere person and a guy who seems to be pulled in all directions because of his superstar status, but that area of his life has not changed.

He knows what his position means and how he can affect so many people, people who don't always have the means to take care of themselves. He's doing a great thing, even if you don't hear much about it.

Former Cardinals pitcher Woody Williams once said about Albert, "At the rate he's going, the day's probably going to come when nobody can compare with Albert Pujols." No less of a baseball expert than Hall of Fame manager Sparky Anderson said, "He's as gifted a hitter as I've seen come along in a long, long time. Before he's done, we might be saying he's the best of them all."

That day is coming very soon.

—John Rooney has been the Cardinals'
radio broadcaster since 2006.

Universally admired in baseball for his intelligence, skill, and approach to hitting, even when Pujols makes an out it usually results in a hard-hit ball.

Pujols bats against the Pirates' Charlie Morton at PNC Park in Pittsburgh on August 8, 2009.

Growing Up to Play Ball

Almost from the time he could walk, Albert Pujols had either a baseball or a bat in his hand. It is true that sometimes the ball was a lime, and sometimes the bat was a stick, and his glove was made from a milk carton, but he was still playing the same game.

Jose Alberto Pujols was born on January 16, 1980, in Santo Domingo, Dominican Republic. He was no different than thousands of other poor young boys in the Caribbean country who fell in love with baseball and took to the streets and dusty fields to play almost every day.

When the young Pujols was not playing the game, he was watching—either his father, Bienvenido, or on television, usually the Atlanta Braves.

Bienvenido Pujols was in demand across the Dominican as an outstanding softball pitcher. The young Pujols often wore his father's jerseys and accompanied him to his games as often as possible. Unfortunately, when the games were over, Pujols' father usually enjoyed more than a few drinks with his friends, and it became his son's responsibility—at the age of 10—to get them safely back home.

A painter by trade, Bienvenido often struggled to find work, and when he did get a job, he could be away from home for some time. The family often lived on government assistance. An only child, Pujols' parents divorced when he was three years old. The father and son moved in with his paternal grandmother, America, and many of her other 10 children also lived in the three-bedroom house. His many aunts and uncles became like brothers and sisters to Pujols.

While watching the Braves' games on television, Pujols was really watching for all the Latin players, players such as Julio Franco, Sammy Sosa, and Raul Mondesi, who quickly became his heroes. He became a student of the game even at an early age, wanting to learn about Latin greats such as Roberto Clemente, Juan Marichal, and others. "All those guys opened the door for us," Pujols says.

Even though he was poor, Pujols does not remember those days with a negative attitude.

"We got our food, and that was the most important thing back then," he says. "My dad always worked hard to get whatever I needed in baseball and to support me. It was a poor country, that's why you can't forget, and it keeps you humble."

Demonstrating the sweet swing that would make him a legend in St. Louis, and indeed all of baseball, Pujols is shown batting for the Potomac Cannons in September 2000 at Pfitzner Stadium in Woodbridge, Virginia.

It did not take long for Pujols' baseball ability to begin to separate him from some of the other youngsters in his community. Scouts, always combing the tiny island country because of its ability to produce baseball superstars, started inviting him to camps to see how he would perform against better competition.

When he was 16, both the Florida Marlins and Oakland A's invited him to their camps, but both declined to offer him a contract. Pujols was disappointed, because by then he was old enough to realize that baseball might provide him with a way to make a better life for himself and his family.

Several of Pujols' relatives already had left the Dominican Republic by then, and were living in New York. America, her son Bienvenido, and grandson Alberto decided to join them in the summer of 1996.

The three did not stay in New York for long. America thought the city was too expensive and too violent, and her thoughts were confirmed about a month after they had moved. She sent Alberto to the grocery store, but on the way he witnessed a shooting only a few feet away from where he was standing. When he got home and told his grandmother, her mind was convinced that New York was no place for them.

Some members of the Pujols family also had left the Dominican Republic and settled outside of Kansas City, Missouri, in the suburb of Independence, where they had found jobs working as school bus drivers. The family convinced America that it was a better place for her, her son, and her grandson to live.

The biggest challenge the move meant for Pujols was that nobody in the community, except his family, spoke Spanish. And Pujols did not speak or understand one word of English.

He enrolled as a sophomore at Fort Osage High School, even though he was a year older than his classmates,

(above) Major league scouts scour the Dominican Republic at youth baseball camps in the hopes of signing the next hot prospect. Multiple teams took a look at Pujols but decided to pass, a decision they surely regret. (opposite) From the time he was a toddler, there was no doubt that Pujols was born to play baseball. A natural, watching other Latin American players success drove Pujols' dream to play major league baseball.

because of his deficiency in English. He was assigned to a tutor, Portia Stanke, an English teacher at the high school. She worked with him every day, and despite Pujols occasionally becoming frustrated and exhausted, she saw the same dedication and determination to succeed at learning the new language as Pujols displayed on the baseball field.

One of the first people Pujols met at his new school was Dave Fry, the baseball coach. Pujols' cousin Wilfredo walked into Fry's science class and introduced his cousin. Fry naturally still remembers that first encounter. With his cousin as his interpreter, Pujols said, "I want to play baseball."

"He was tall and good looking, with big shoulders and a little waist," Fry says. "I told him, 'If you want to play, we're going to have a tryout session in February.' I didn't think about him anymore."

That quickly changed, however, when Fry soon became one of the first people to learn that the baseball just has a different sound when it is coming off Pujols' bat.

"I heard this 'whack, whack, whack' and I thought, 'What in the world?'" Fry recalls. "I went and took a look, and Albert was in the cage, lining some shots. 'Gee boy, what have we got here?' I said. "He was a man among boys."

Fry quickly learned that despite Pujols' inability to speak or understand English, the language of baseball is universal.

"Most of the time I would act it out or show him what I was trying to get across," Fry said. "He would keep me up all night taking ground balls, but his forte was hitting.

"Language was Albert's biggest barrier. He had trouble understanding when you explained rules and regulations to him. But he loved baseball. You could get anything about baseball through to him, how to move his hands when he hit, where to set his feet when he was fielding."

The only minor suggestion Fry said he ever made to Pujols about hitting was that he might find it helpful to

(above) Baseball is not a spoken language, and Pujols always stood at the top of the heap once it came time to take the field. He is always ready for a light moment, as seen here with Jose Reyes during the 2006 NLCS. (opposite) His swing may be a sight to behold today, but hitting has always come naturally for Pujols. He was known for his big stick in high school, batting .471 in his first season.

lower his hands a little instead of holding his bat so high.

"Everything was natural for him," Fry said. "You only had to see Albert swing the bat once or twice to notice that he had some pretty good power. I never saw a kid swing so hard on every pitch. Not just once in a while, but every pitch. At our school, we have a short left field porch, and he constantly bombarded that house behind the fence."

Pujols played shortstop, and as a sophomore, led Fort Osage to the 1997 Missouri Class 4A state championship. He hit .471 with 11 homers and 32 RBIs.

"Albert was always so proud to wear his baseball uniform to class the day he had a game," Stanke said. "But when he came back the next day, he never bragged. You only knew if you asked him."

Opposing coaches, however, quickly learned all about Pujols. During his junior year, perhaps as an indication of what was to come many years later, Pujols walked an incredible 55 times in just 88 plate appearances. In the 33 times he did get to bat, he slugged eight homers.

Fry still remembers one particular blast, at visiting Liberty High School. The ball landed on top of a 25-foot-tall air-conditioning unit, which sat on the roof of a building about 40 feet beyond the outfield fence. Estimates by observers were that the ball traveled at least 450 feet.

Fry was as frustrated as Pujols with the opponent's strategy, which also became kind of an unwritten protest by coaches who questioned whether Pujols was actually older than his listed age.

"They would let him bat one time and then walk him," Fry said. "Albert got pretty fed up with that. But if I was the opponent, I would have done it too."

Ryan Wood played for Lee's Summit North High School, a conference opponent of Fort Osage, and admitted that his team did not like facing Pujols.

"We had a sophomore playing third base for us, and he was scared to death," Wood recalled. "Pujols was built like a man already, and with a metal bat in his hand, it was a scary thing. We made it a point to pitch to him if nobody was on base or if first base was occupied, but otherwise we didn't want to mess with him."

Wood also faced Pujols in American Legion games and remembers one playoff game in particular.

"He had had his wisdom teeth taken out that morning, and he didn't start the game," Wood said. "We thought we were going to get a break. We were up something like 15–10, and he came off the bench as a pinch-hitter and hit a screaming line drive over the right field fence for a three-run homer. We still ended up winning the game, but he just showed he was so talented that things like taking out his wisdom teeth did not get in his way. It was a privilege to watch him play."

Despite his offensive success, Pujols did not make the high school all-metro team, selected by the *Kansas City Star,* during either of his sophomore or junior seasons. As a junior, he was picked to the *Star*'s second team, behind Ryan Stegall of Liberty. The biggest reason for the slight was Pujols' defense—he committed more than 20 errors, most of them on wild throws.

"We were trying to get Albert to field the ball, go from the ground to the gut, point the shoulders, and step and throw," Fry said. "That's a lot of things to say."

Even though Pujols was only a junior, professional scouts began to notice what he was accomplishing on the field. The scouts could tell that he would not be a shortstop as he got older, but they had trouble projecting

Pujols' infectious passion for the game has shone through his entire life, pushing others to work harder to try and keep up. His incredible work ethic was a plus for the scouts that saw him, though the neighbors near the fences of his high school outfield had to bear some punishment.

where the best position for him to play would be.

Playing only a few miles from the home of the Kansas City Royals, the team's scouts had plenty of opportunity to watch Pujols but came to the same conclusions as most other teams...he simply was too young to project what kind of player he could become. Even though he was 18 by then, he was not eligible for the 1998 draft because his class had not graduated.

"We all saw Albert about the same way," said Allard Baird, a former general manager of the Royals. "We weren't sure he had a position. He didn't have a great baseball body. We all saw him the same way, and we were all wrong."

A coach for his summer league team, Russ Meyer, was even a part-time scout for the Royals.

"I wrote in my report that I thought he had the potential to be drafted between the third and fifth round,"

Meyer said. "Turns out that I underestimated him too."

Herk Robinson, the Royals' general manager, said the team had an even closer connection to Pujols than they realized.

"We had someone in our engineering department who actually lived with Albert for about three months," Robinson said. "You can't get much more in your backyard than that."

The area scout for the Cardinals, Dave Karaff, was the brother-in-law of Mike Roberts, a scouting supervisor for the team. Roberts read Karaff's reports and first saw Pujols for himself at the Area Code Games the summer after his junior season.

"The first thing you noticed about him was his strength," Roberts said. "He was not as big physically as he is now, but you could tell that he could hit."

One scout was not impressed with Pujols, Roberts

(above) The Kansas City Royals had a better chance than most teams to get a good look at Pujols, though they, too, decided to take a pass on him. Today, all they can do is try to contain him, such as with this intentional walk. (opposite) Scouts everywhere missed out on Pujols, including one that was unimpressed with the prospect's speed. While he's no speedster on the bags, Pujols had a career-high 17 stolen bases in 2005.

said, adding that "the only thing he wrote down on his report was 4.7, the time he ran going to first base."

"He was not the kind of player that was going to blow you away when you first saw him," Roberts said. "I just saw size and strength."

Aware of his desire to play professional baseball, many scouts talked to Pujols and advised him that his best chance to get teams interested would be to leave high school early, skipping his senior season. Their rationale was that teams would pitch him the same way that year as they had his junior year, walking him multiple times and giving him little chance to hit and display his ability.

Pujols thought the idea made perfect sense, so he arranged to graduate from Fort Osage midway through his senior season. He had met Marty Kilgore, the coach at nearby Maple Woods Community College, at an all-star game in the Kansas City area, and Kilgore was able to convince him to enroll at the school in January 1999.

It did not take long for Pujols to make the same impression on Kilgore as he had made on Fry when he joined the high school team. All it took was listening to the difference when Pujols began to hit.

"You don't hear that kind of explosion often," Kilgore said.

One of Pujols' new teammates, Landon Brandes, was a sophomore and had been the team's leading hitter until Pujols arrived. Brandes, who went on to play in the Cardinals' farm system, remembered that day very clearly.

"Everyone was using metal bats," Brandes said. "Albert stepped in with a wood bat. I was hitting some out of the park before that, and I felt pretty good."

Pujols, with the wooden bat, hit the ball an estimated 50 feet farther than the balls Brandes had hit with a metal bat. "Are you kidding me?" Brandes remembers thinking. "This kid is right out of high school and he's outblasting me?"

As debuts go, Pujols' first game for Maple Woods was pretty good. All he did was turn an unassisted triple play at shortstop and hit a grand slam. It was the start of a season that would see him hit .461 with 22 homers and 80 RBIs.

Like the memorable home runs Pujols hit in high school, people still talk about some of Pujols' blasts for Maple Woods. Playing at Highland, Kansas Community College, Pujols hit a homer that cleared the fence, cleared the street behind the fence, and landed in a tree.

He did not homer on another blast—into a 30-mile per hour wind—and had to settle for a triple.

"He was pretty mad about it," Kilgore said. "He didn't think the wind should have mattered."

It was more than Pujols' ability to hit tape-measure home runs that impressed Kilgore, however.

"He had baseball instincts that just couldn't be taught," Kilgore said. "The way he would run the bases, going from second to third when a third baseman came up throwing...just knowing how much to get off so they wouldn't throw behind him...just the little things you can't teach that made him a special player. He was the best athlete I've ever seen with the baseball skills and power."

As could be expected, word of Pujols' ability spread to Maple Woods' opponents. One team from Seminole, Oklahoma, developed the unconventional strategy of hitting Pujols and Brandes with pitches every time they came up to bat.

"Every time they hit Albert, he would just stand there, look at them, and stare them down," Kilgore said.

Pujols launches yet another tape-measure home run into the seats at Busch Stadium. His prodigious power displays have always awed fans, but it's the completeness of his game that has won him so many admirers inside baseball.

"Nothing scares him."

Pujols led Maple Woods to the NJCAA regional championship, falling just one game short of earning a trip to the national World Series.

Karaff, and other scouts, had watched how Pujols had continued to improve against the stronger competition but still were unsure about projecting a professional future.

The first time Karaff brought in a Cardinals' cross-checker to watch Pujols, he struck out twice—the first time Karaff had ever seen Pujols strike out on a fastball. In another at-bat, Pujols tripped over first base running out a ground ball.

"Luckily for me the scout came back the next day, too, and saw him hit one out of sight," Karaff said.

Another scout who had taken a liking to Pujols was Fernando Arango, who worked for the Tampa Bay Devil Rays. "It wasn't fair with him using an aluminum bat," Arango said. "When he hit the ball it sounded like thunder."

Arango, who had Pujols ranked as the top prospect in his scouting area, convinced his bosses to bring Pujols to St. Petersburg for a workout prior to the amateur draft. The day did not get off to a good start, when the Rays' officials asked Pujols to put on catching gear and work out behind the plate.

"Albert was very upset about that," Arango said. "He didn't want to do it."

Pujols, who knew his most logical position in pro baseball was either at first base or third base, hit the ball hard during the tryout but did not launch any tape-measure home runs. He did hit one ball off the top of

(above) It was hard to project where Pujols might play in the major leagues, but it was for certain that he could play the corners of the infield. One team, at least, asked him to even put on the catcher's gear. **(opposite)** There was one sure commodity with Pujols as a prospect: he could hit the ball a mile. One blast at a Tampa workout hit the very top of the left field foul pole.

the left field foul pole, Arango said.

Arango thought Pujols would be drafted in the second or third round. Karaff and Mike Roberts were more conservative, listing him as a probable choice somewhere between the sixth and 10th round, given his relatively brief experience in high school and junior college and the uncertainty about what position would be best for him.

"He moved okay, and he had a good enough arm that I thought he could maybe play third base," Roberts said. "I knew for sure he ought to be able to play first. What I saw I liked, but I knew what was going to carry him was his bat. I thought if he hit we could find a position for him to play.

"He was actually a better hitter with a wood bat than he was with an aluminum bat. He stayed back on the ball better. In the games, he would drive some balls, but he also struck out some."

Roberts was in the draft room on that June day in 1999 when Tampa Bay made Josh Hamilton the first pick in the draft. The Cardinals did not pick until the 30th turn, a compensatory pick from Atlanta for losing free agent Brian Jordan. The team chose Chance Caple, a right-handed pitcher from Texas A&M who never made it out of the minor leagues.

Through 12 rounds, the Cardinals, Rays, and every other team passed on Pujols. After the 10th round, Roberts began to lobby his bosses to consider Pujols. Finally, on the 13th round, after 401 other players had been selected, the Cardinals took Pujols.

"We were lucky," Roberts admits. "I think we got him because I happened to be there and had a chance to talk about him in the room. The area scout (Karaff) wasn't there, but because we had somebody who liked him there at the end, we were able to take him."

Pujols was disappointed that he had been selected so low and actually considered giving up the game he loved. "It did bother me, I won't lie," Pujols said years later. "I was disappointed."

So was Arango, the Tampa scout who actually thought maybe he had been wrong in his evaluation. "This guy didn't go in the first round, second round, or third round," Arango said. "I thought, 'If I can't get him drafted in the 13th round, then something is wrong. It could be me.'"

Time has proven there was nothing wrong with Arango's scouting ability.

Still upset and undecided about his future, Pujols rejected the Cardinals' initial contract offer and moved to Hays, Kansas, to play on a collegiate summer league team. He moved in with the coach, Frank Leo, and his wife Barb.

"He was so aware of everything," Leo said, "how to hit certain kinds of pitchers, how to run the bases, how to play every situation. He came to us with a purpose in mind. He had a goal, and he wasn't going to be distracted from it."

One of the reasons Pujols had been hoping to become a high draft pick was financial. He had fallen in love with a woman, Deidre Corona, whom he had met at Cashmere, a Latin dance club in Kansas City. Pujols was just 18 at the time, even though the minimum age to enter the club was 21. Pujols eventually worked up the nerve to ask her for her phone number, then admitted he had a confession to make...he was not 21.

Deidre asked if he was 22 or maybe even 23. When he replied that he was 18, she was stunned. "You're barely legal," she said.

The age difference initially bothered Deidre, who had

Pujols, the National League Rookie of the Year, is shown during a news conference in November 2001. The 21-year-old Pujols, a unanimous choice for the award, set an NL rookie record with 130 RBIs and led the Cardinals with a .329 average, 37 homers, and 112 runs.

Pujols signs an autograph for a young fan with Down syndrome in 2003. Pujols has always been keenly aware of those in need, and has had sympathy for others throughout his life.

grown up in the Kansas City area and had graduated from Kansas State. She was working three jobs. After the couple continued to talk, over dinner at the Cheesecake Factory, Deidre said she had something to tell Pujols too—she was a single mother with an eight-month-old daughter, Isabella.

A week later, after that news had not scared Pujols away, Deidre told him that Isabella had been born with Down syndrome. Still, the news did not keep Pujols from wanting to be with Deidre. She gave him some literature in Spanish so he would better understand Isabella's condition.

Pujols often babysat for the young child when Deidre was at work. She helped him with his English and got him a part-time job at a pizzeria. Pujols gave the money he earned to Deidre. She soon knew their relationship was meant to be.

"Albert never went to clubs," she said. "He did not drink. He didn't even want people smoking around him.

He wasn't even old enough to be in the place."

It was actually a pep talk from Deidre's mother, Linda Corona, that convinced Pujols to stop worrying about where he had been selected in the draft.

"I said, 'Albert, go. You love to play. You will prove yourself when you get there.'"

Pujols listened.

"I prayed about it," he said. "God blessed me and gave me the chance. I decided I didn't care too much about where I got drafted. I knew if I was good enough, I would make it to the big leagues in three or four years."

Karaff finally got Pujols' signature on a contract at the end of the summer in 1999, giving Pujols a $65,000 signing bonus and extra money if he decided to go back to college.

"He was such a great kid," Karaff said. "I really liked him. I knew he wanted to play, and we finally got it done."

Pujols' dream of becoming a professional baseball player was about to come true. ■

(above) Always a student of the game, Pujols studies opposing pitchers even on his off days. His willingness to absorb information and adapt his game to the circumstances around him has helped him since his earliest days playing. (opposite) Pujols' family has stood by him since before he was drafted, from his wife, Deidre, to his son, A.J., and daughter, Sophia, seen here in the closing days of the old Busch Stadium.

A moment with a Hall of Famer—early in his rookie year, Pujols sits down with the legendary Jack Buck for a pregame interview.

Welcome to the Majors

Because he signed so late in the 1999 season, Pujols missed the regular minor league year. His first experience as a professional came at the Cardinals' instructional league camp in Jupiter, Florida, in October.

One of the people eager to watch Pujols was Mike Jorgensen, the team's director of player development.

On his first swing during batting practice at Roger Dean Stadium, Pujols blasted a line drive over the left field fence, striking the wall of the Montreal Expos' offices behind the fence. It was not the only long drive Pujols hit that day.

"In spring training you see the big boys popping the ball up there, but usually during the Instructional League you hardly see anybody who can hit it over the fence," said Jorgensen, who was watching from the stands.

As he continued to watch Pujols over the next several days, Jorgensen was left with a question for anybody he could ask.

"How come he wasn't drafted until the 13th round?" Jorgensen wanted to know. "I was told some scouts thought he was heavy and didn't move

that well, but everybody had to see the bat. It stood out that much. A lot of teams missed the boat, but we were lucky to get him."

Pujols knew he would be playing minor league baseball somewhere in the Cardinals' system in 2000, and he did not want to face that challenge alone. On New Year's Day 2000, he and Deidre were married.

With his personal life exactly where he wanted it, Pujols was free to concentrate on baseball. After spring training, the Cardinals assigned him to their Class A team in the Midwest League, the Peoria Chiefs. His manager was Tom Lawless, a former major league infielder.

"We knew he needed work on defense, but you could tell he was an outstanding hitter," Lawless said. "His mechanics were so good that he was taking the pitch from the middle of the plate out and hitting it to right center and right field. That is usually a skill you have to teach young hitters; they normally try to pull everything.

"As the pitchers began to scout him, they started to work him inside more, and he was still trying to hit the pitch the other way. We had to

Less than two months into his major league career, Pujols was already being summoned for curtain calls by the Busch Stadium faithful. The eighth-inning homer that brought the fans to their feet helped put the Milwaukee Brewers away.

teach him to get the barrel of the bat through the zone quicker so he could pull that pitch to left field. It didn't take him long to figure it out.

"I knew he was on his way. He has such strong hands, and his hand-eye coordination is so good, that was the secret to his success."

Pujols was playing so well in fact that when Mitchell Page, then the organization's minor-league roving hitting instructor came to town, he left Pujols' name off the list of players he thought needed some extra work.

Pujols was upset that his name was omitted.

"He wasn't happy hitting .330 or .340 in A ball," Page said, "so I gave him all the work he wanted."

The question wasn't about his hitting—that was good enough for him to make the league's All-Star team. The concern was finding him a position, and all involved thought third base was the most likely spot.

"Once he figured it out there was no question he would hit in the big leagues," Lawless said. "I thought he probably could have hit in the big leagues then, but he needed somewhere to play."

Lawless and other instructors spent a great deal of time teaching Pujols the position.

"He was a very good student," Lawless said. "He worked hard and wanted to learn. He had the same problems a lot of young players have when he got frustrated and didn't run out some ground balls. We had a little chat and took care of that. I told him, 'Don't make yourself look bad.' He was a good kid.

"It was his first year in pro baseball, and he didn't really know what to expect, but he was very professional about how he went about his business."

For the first time in his life, Pujols was being paid to play baseball. But his take-home salary of $242 every two weeks was barely enough to pay for a sparsely furnished apartment for his young family and to keep food on the table.

(opposite) This high fly ball went foul in 2001, but later in the at-bat Pujols singled home J.D. Drew to tie the franchise record for RBIs by a rookie, which was first set in 1953. (above) Pujols adapted well to the life of a professional. It only took him one season of minor league ball before advancing to the majors, where he soon found himself a part of a pennant race.

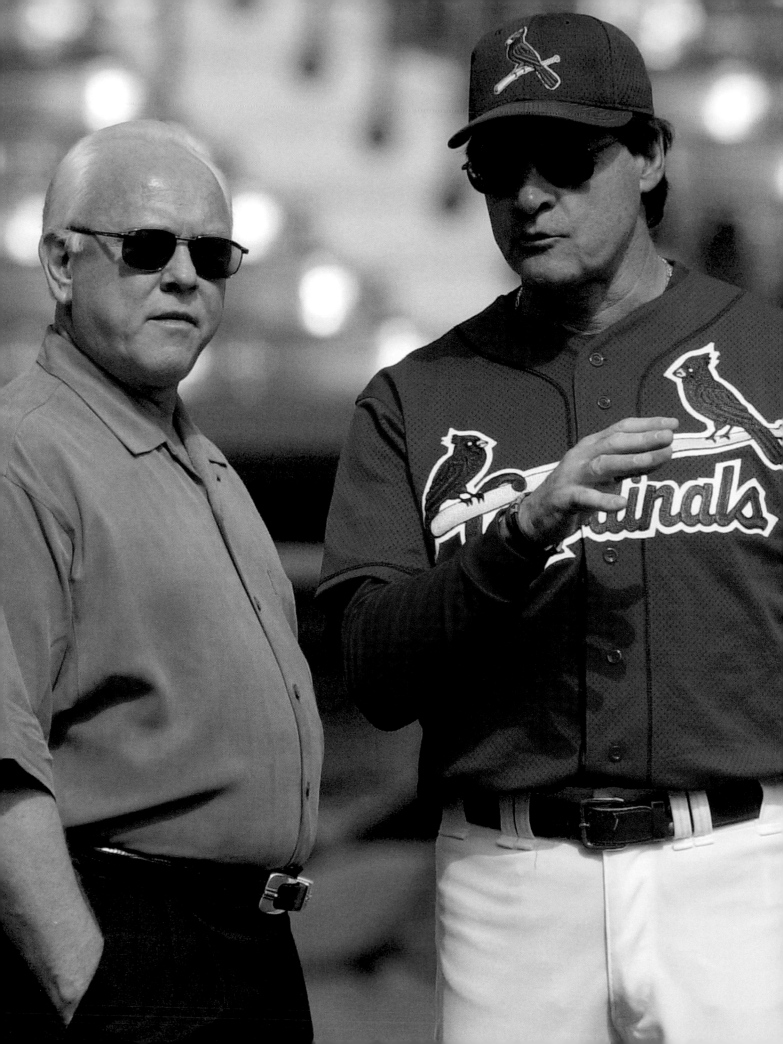

He still dreamed of the day he would play in the major leagues and have all of the comforts available to players at that level. Because Peoria was only a few hours north of St. Louis, Pujols was able to attend some Cardinals games at Busch Stadium on his days off, sitting in the stands.

Elsewhere at the stadium, word of Pujols' performance was spreading. One of his teammates at Peoria was Chris Duncan, the son of the Cardinals' pitching coach Dave Duncan, and the two regularly discussed Pujols' accomplishments. Jorgensen was also watching Pujols, as he was all of the organization's prospects.

Near the end of July, the major league club wanted to add a backup catcher to its roster and began talking with the San Diego Padres about Carlos Hernandez. The Padres had an area scout who lived near Peoria and watched a lot of their games, and he recommended that his team ask for either Pujols or a young outfielder, Ben Johnson, in the trade.

"Pujols was still a little bit of a secret even though people knew about his numbers," Jorgensen said. "Johnson's numbers were not quite as good, but we liked him a lot too. We didn't want to trade either one of them, but we needed a backup catcher. We traded Johnson."

Johnson, as Jorgensen predicted, did become a major league player but not a star at that level.

Pujols likely didn't even know his name had come up in trade discussions, but he soon was also on the move—earning a promotion to the Cardinals' high Class A team in Woodbridge, Virginia.

Pujols left Peoria with a .324 average, 17 homers, and 84 RBIs in 109 games. Showing the plate discipline he would continue to display for the rest of his career, Pujols struck out only 37 times in 395 at-bats.

It was a good enough performance to earn him the league's Most Valuable Player award, and he and a player

(above) On his days off in the minors, Pujols headed down the road a few hours to catch the big club in action. He sat in the stands, thinking about the day when he would join the players on the field at Busch Stadium. (opposite) Walt Jocketty, senior vice president and general manager for the St. Louis Cardinals. and manager Tony La Russa, shown here in 2002, quickly recognized they had something special when Pujols started posting eye-popping numbers in their minor league system.

After being a one-man wrecking crew throughout the Cardinals minor league system, Pujols continued his success at the major league level. Here, he celebrates a grand slam late in his rookie season.

in the Reds' system, outfielder Austin Kearns, shared the honor as the league's top major league prospect.

Among the fans watching Pujols' first game in Potomac was Walt Jocketty, the Cardinals' general manager.

"He came to bat with runners in scoring position," Jocketty said. "I think he was behind in the count 1–2, and he hit the next pitch up the middle for an RBI. Same thing with his next at-bat, in an almost identical situation. I said, 'Man, this guy just gets off a plane, and he already is an RBI machine.'"

In 21 games at Potomac before the end of the season, Pujols hit .284 with two homers and 10 RBIs. One of his teammates who was impressed was future Cardinals second baseman Bo Hart.

"He hit the ball harder and more often than anyone I had ever seen," Hart said. "Anytime he made an out, it just seemed like someone accidentally was there to catch the ball."

Pujols likely thought his year was coming to an end, but the Cardinals had other ideas. Memphis outfielder Ernie Young had left the Triple A team to join the U.S. Olympic team, and manager Gaylen Pitts told Jorgensen he would like to add a right-handed hitter who could come off the bench during the Pacific Coast League playoffs.

When Pitts suggested that Pujols be promoted to Memphis, Jorgensen was hesitant to agree. Pitts finally convinced him, and Pujols arrived at the Triple A level in time to play the last three games of the regular season.

After getting just three hits in 14 at-bats in those games, Pujols caught fire in the playoffs. In 11 postseason games he hit .302 and capped the performance with a game and pennant-winning homer in the 13th inning of the deciding game against Salt Lake City. Pujols was named the playoffs' MVP.

"He was kind of a one-man wrecking crew," Jorgensen said. "By then you could tell he was going to be

(opposite) With his odyssey through the minors complete, Pujols was excited to see major league pitching. There was little doubt he was ready—the question for the Cardinals was how to get him at-bats on a solid team. (above) One of the people most impressed with Pujols during his days in the minor leagues was general manager Walt Jocketty. In 2004, he rewarded the first baseman with a $100 million contract.

a special player and not just a special hitter. I really have to give a lot of credit to Pitts for wanting him and giving him a chance at that level."

Pujols' next stop was in Scottsdale, Arizona, in the Arizona Fall League, a place where organizations annually send their top prospects. In 27 games he hit .323 with four homers and 21 RBIs and was voted the league's best third-base prospect.

His first minor league season had been very successful in every way except financially. Needing to make more money in the winter, Pujols went to work at Meadowbrook Country Club in Kansas City, setting up rooms for parties and other functions. His family moved in with his in-laws, and when he was not working, he was at the gym, hitting and working out, trying to get ready for the next baseball season.

As he reported to spring training, Pujols knew the Cardinals' plan was likely for him to begin the year in Memphis, still a big jump from where he had played for most of 2000, skipping the Double A level. In his mind, however, Pujols had already proven that he could compete and succeed at that level—he thought he was ready for the major leagues.

Pujols was assigned uniform number 68, a pretty good indication that nobody was expecting him to make the major league roster. Two established veterans, Placido Polanco and Craig Paquette, were projected to split most of the playing time at third base.

The camp was not very far along, however, when Pujols began opening some eyes.

"He was taking really professional at-bats," said Dave Duncan, who couldn't help but notice Pujols while he was trying to watch his pitchers get in their early work.

"You could tell he was determined to compete, even in those situations. He wasn't going to do something in the cage in February that was going to create a bad habit or give a bad impression."

Manager Tony La Russa also noticed the young prospect, and injuries to Mark McGwire and Bobby Bonilla gave him a chance to write Pujols into the lineup, at either third base, first base, or in the outfield. The more chances that Pujols received, the bigger an impression he was starting to make.

"It was impossible to get him to perform poorly, and I pushed him," La Russa said. "Dave Duncan accused me of trying to find a place where he couldn't play, but Albert refused to cooperate. I kept using him against the toughest pitchers, and he kept hitting."

With about 10 days left in camp, Pujols was not in the lineup for a game against the Braves. McGwire asked La Russa if Pujols was going to make the team, and La Russa admitted he really did not think there would be a place for him to play—and he didn't want him sitting on the bench when he could be playing everyday at Triple A.

In the ninth inning, La Russa called on Pujols to pinch-hit...and he slammed a home run over the scoreboard in centerfield. McGwire was standing next to La Russa in the dugout and dug his elbow into La Russa's side. "How are you not going to take him?" McGwire asked.

The answer came when Bonilla suffered a pulled hamstring, opening a spot and a position. Pujols finished the spring with a .349 average and a team-leading 34 total bases. Perhaps even more impressive, in his first exposure to major-league pitching, was the fact that he struck out only eight times in 62 at-bats.

When La Russa informed Pujols that he indeed

Pujols is greeted by teammates after scoring against the Phillies on Opening Day 2006 in Philadelphia.

would be on the Opening Day roster, he did so with a cautionary warning ... his spot was not secure past the opening weekend. When Bonilla was ready to come off the disabled list, another roster move would have to be made.

Pujols understood, but as he traded in his number 68 jersey for one with a more conventional number, 5, he hoped such a move would not be necessary.

The Cardinals opened the regular season on April 2 in Denver, against the Colorado Rockies, and just 361 days after he had made his professional debut in Class A, Pujols found himself in the starting lineup, playing left field and batting sixth.

Also at Coors Field that day, either by fate or coincidence, was the greatest player in Cardinals history—Stan Musial. He was in Denver attending a card show and came to the park just to watch the game.

What he saw was nothing historic or memorable. Pujols did record the first hit of his major league career, a single to center off Mike Hampton in the seventh inning. It was one of only five hits the Cardinals managed against Hampton, who won 8–0.

Pujols remained in the lineup for the next two days but went hitless. Most rookies who started out one for nine—when they already had been told their spot in the roster was tenuous—would be a little concerned. Most rookies did not include Pujols.

"I was hitting the ball good, so I didn't get frustrated," he said. "I knew what I could do."

La Russa kept Pujols in the lineup when the Cardinals arrived in Phoenix to play the Diamondbacks. All he did was lead the team to a sweep of the three-game series, going seven-for-14 with eight RBIs and his first major league homer, off Armando Reynoso.

His biggest at-bat of the series, however, came in the final game against future Hall of Famer Randy Johnson—a two-out, two-strike double that once

(opposite) Batting .349 in his first spring training earned a roster spot for Pujols. Though he struggled through his first series, he would soon adjust and thrive. (above) After spending his first spring training wearing the number 68, Pujols switched to the now-familiar 5 when he made the Cardinals roster.

again left McGwire shaking his head.

"When he bombed the double off the wall in center field off Randy Johnson, we all went, 'Uh-oh, we've got something here,'" McGwire said.

The Cardinals then headed to St. Louis for their home opener, against Colorado, and Pujols became the team's first rookie since Wally Moon in 1953 to homer in the home opener.

"After grounding out in my first at-bat of the season, I said to myself, 'Okay, just relax and play the game like you always do,'" Pujols said. "That's what I'm doing."

When Bonilla was ready to play, the temporary pass La Russa had given Pujols was forgotten. John Mabry was designated for assignment, and his contract was sold to Florida. Pujols finished April with eight homers, tying the major league record for homers in that month by a rookie. For the month he hit .370 and had 27 RBIs in 24 games.

What impressed his teammates, however, was that Pujols still was not satisfied with his performance.

"He's the type of kid who will sit next to you and ask questions," said veteran Larry Sutton. "He doesn't act presumptuous. He doesn't act like he's been in the big leagues for 10 years. He's in the cage 24 hours a day and wants to get better. That's all you can ask for from a young player."

One opposing manager who still had some doubts about Pujols' ability was Arizona's Bob Brenly.

"We just don't know the kid," Brenly said. "The series we had in Arizona, we just had bad scouting reports. We ended up throwing the ball right where he likes it, a lot. That being said, we went back and watched the tape, and he also hit some good pitches.

"He's obviously a physically gifted young man. A lot of rookies come up at this level and feel overmatched. They're not sure if they belong or can compete at this level. Other rookies come up with that little edge, that confidence, that look in their eye that they belong. He certainly has that look."

(opposite) Towards the end of a rookie season for the ages, there were plenty of occasions for Pujols to make a curtain call. On this day, it was the breaking of the club's rookie RBI record, a mark that had stood since 1953. (above) One can only imagine what Mark McGwire and Albert Pujols could have accomplished had they been in their primes at the same time. In 2001, the younger slugger congratulates the older player, who had just hit a three-run dinger.

As the season continued and teams had more of a scouting report on Pujols, they still found out how hard it was to pitch to him. He hit .333 in May, with eight more homers, and .330 in June, with five homers.

One person who immediately was impressed was Cardinals hitting coach Mike Easler, who correctly predicted early in 2001 that "people are going to be paying just to see Albert Pujols one day."

"Only a few guys can make that sound," Easler said of Pujols' hitting ability. "Willie Stargell, Dave Parker, Dave Winfield, Mike Schmidt. I'm talking about guys like that. The ball just explodes off his bat, and he's talented enough that he can take his power swing and make adjustments and go the other way for a base hit.

"I can tell him something in between at-bats about how a pitcher is trying to work him, and he can make the adjustments just that quick. The next at-bat, he'll do exactly what you've talked to him about. It's just amazing how polished he is at such a young age."

Not even the first prolonged slump of his career—a 2-for-33 slide in early July—could keep him off the NL All-Star team, the first Cardinals rookie chosen for the game since pitcher Luis Arroyo in 1955. When he entered the game as a replacement for Jeff Kent at second base, he became the first Cardinals rookie to actually play in the All-Star Game since Eddie Kazak in 1949. He walked in his only plate appearance.

His offensive consistency—his 21 home runs at the break already tied the team rookie record for a season, set by Ray Jablonski in 1953—was even more impressive considering he was moving all over the field, starting at least two games at five different positions.

A 20–10 month in August moved the Cardinals into the division and wild card races, led by Pujols' continued offensive assault. On August 29 he hit his 31st homer of the year and reached the 100 RBI mark, the first rookie to do so for the franchise since Jablonski.

It was a foregone conclusion in September that he would be the Rookie of the Year, but talk was building that he might be in line for an even higher honor, the MVP award.

"I really believe the stats don't come anywhere close to telling the story of how this guy's played," La Russa said. "He's been able to maintain this for six months. I don't care if you've been in the league 10 years, he's had a phenomenal season.

"I've been fortunate and had some MVP performances. I think of Carlton Fisk, Harold Baines, Jose Canseco, Mark McGwire, Rickey Henderson. But I don't know anybody who has had a better year than this guy. He's been as good as any I've been fortunate to see. What this kid has done is the greatest performance of any position player I've ever seen."

The Cardinals and Astros finished tied for first place with matching 93–69 records, but the Astros were awarded the division title because of the better record in their head-to-head matchups. The Cardinals advanced to the playoffs, against Arizona, as the wild card team.

Even though Pujols struggled in that series—going 2-for-18 as the Cardinals were eliminated in the fifth and deciding game by the eventual World Series champions—what he had accomplished in his rookie season would not be forgotten for a long time.

He led the Cardinals in all three Triple Crown categories—batting average (.329), homers (37), and RBIs (130)—the first Cardinals rookie to record that feat since

After rocking a big hit off Randy Johnson in just the second series of the season, Pujols hammered the Arizona ace hard again in October. Unfortunately, this two-run blast in the first inning of the NLDS Game 2 was not enough to carry the Cards past the Diamondbacks.

Hall of Famer Rogers Hornsby did it in 1916 and the first Cardinal to do it at any stage of their career since Ted Simmons in 1973.

Pujols became one of only four rookies in history, and the first in the National League, to hit .300 with 30 homers, 100 RBIs, and 100 runs scored and the first to do it since Boston's Walt Dropo in 1950. The only other players to do it were Hal Trotsky in 1934 and Ted Williams in 1939. Pujols also became the first Cardinal in that exclusive club since Musial did it in 1952.

"Everything about Albert is legitimate," La Russa said. "He could do this for a long time. The two biggest issues that could get in the way of him having a great career are first, that he's a big guy. We saw in spring training that he had a really good winter training and stayed in shape. He was quick. The older you get, the tougher it is to carry weight. So he will have to keep up that kind of work.

"Second, maybe most important, is the atmosphere today in the major leagues that if a guy is successful, even if he is just a little successful, much less incredibly successful, he will face a lot of pressure."

When the postseason awards were handed out, Pujols was a unanimous choice as the league's Rookie of the Year, only the ninth time in history the voting had been unanimous. He also finished fourth in balloting for the MVP.

"I'm not surprised I've had success because I worked hard for this," Pujols said. "God gave me the ability and talent to play this game. He gave me the ability and attitude to respect this game. It wouldn't be right for me to be lazy and take God's gifts for granted."

For that reason, and because of that attitude, Pujols was just as determined as ever to work even harder as he prepared for his second season in the majors. He knew there had been players who had enjoyed very good rookie seasons and then struggled after that, and he was determined not to become one of them. ■

(opposite) Unanimously voted the National League's Rookie of the Year in 2001, Pujols was still not satisfied with his game after his first season. He knew he could improve. (above) Cardinals manager Tony La Russa watches his troops from the dugout. He speaks glowingly of Pujols, seemingly aware that he has never managed a player with as much skill and heart as his first baseman.

Becoming a Star

Pujols could have let the success of his rookie season go to his head and relax, but that was not his style. Many winter mornings, he could be found in the gym by 6:30 AM, working out with teammate Mike Matheny and others.

"I don't want to throw this opportunity away," Pujols said. "I don't want to be lazy in this game. I don't want to be cocky. I don't want to think that I'm the best. I always want to be humble and be the same guy I was three or four years ago, when I signed, through the minor leagues and here in the big leagues."

Pujols knew that one of the reasons he had enjoyed one of the best rookie seasons in the history of the game was because of all of the hard work and preparation he had put it, both before and during the season. He also knew that what had happened last year was now history.

"It's not what you did last year. It's what you're going to do this year," Pujols said. "That's more important."

One of the ways Pujols hoped to actually improve on his performance as a rookie was by studying opposing hitters, as well as pitchers, and

listening when they offered advice. One player who suggested a new drill to Pujols was Alex Rodriguez.

"You look at the best hitters, and you try to learn something from them," Pujols said. "I do that with every team we play. I learn something new every time I walk into a park. You learn from your mistakes and things that happen. Every day, you learn something new, and that's what you want to do to get better and better."

Another motivating factor for Pujols in his second season in the majors was the Cardinals' disappointing loss in the first round of the playoffs the previous year. Pujols had learned very quickly how important it was to win, and having the Cardinals advance further in the playoffs than the first round was one of his, and the team's, goals for 2002.

One of the obstacles that Pujols and his teammates did not count on in trying to meet that goal was having to overcome tragedy. Just five days after the team's legendary broadcaster, Jack Buck, died on June 17, pitcher Darryl Kile was found dead in his Chicago hotel room before the Cardinals were set to play the Cubs.

While Buck had suffered from a long illness,

Motivated by a solid rookie season and a playoff appearance that left him thirsty for more, Pujols was determined to make his team and himself better in 2002.

the death of Kile, at the age of 33, was a stunning blow to the team. Led by Pujols, the team rallied together and developed a motto of "For Darryl" the rest of the season. The team ended the year with 97 victories and a division championship. On the day Kile died, the Cardinals had 40 wins. Kile wore uniform number 57. That did not seem like a mere coincidence.

Pujols hit .335 after the All-Star break and drove in 61 runs, the most in the league, as he once again posted a .300 average and surpassed the 30-homer mark, the 100-RBI plateau, and scored more than 100 runs for the second consecutive year. His success also earned him the runner-up spot to Barry Bonds in the league's MVP voting.

The division title gave Pujols a chance to improve on his playoff performance from 2001. The Cardinals again met Arizona in the first round, and this time swept the Diamondbacks as Pujols hit .300 and drove in three runs. Their opponent in the National League Championship

Series was the Giants, who found a way to limit Pujols to five hits in 19 at-bats, including one homer, as they won the series to the advance to the World Series.

One player who joined the Cardinals that season, and was quickly added to the list of Pujols admirers, was third baseman Scott Rolen, acquired in a trade from the Phillies in July.

"You see him twice a year and you figure you're catching him when he's hot," Rolen said. "When you're on the same team, you realize he's like that every day. You think he has to cool off sometimes, but he doesn't. He's that good.

"He has a knack of controlling the at-bat instead of the pitcher controlling the at-bat. The pitcher needs to make adjustments. The other thing is, he has the ability of knowing where the bat head is and getting the bat head to the ball. Barry (Bonds) hits so many balls on the barrel. That's the way Albert is. You can throw him an inside

(above) Baseball is supposed to be fun, and despite taking the game very seriously, Pujols still knows how to enjoy himself. Here, Pujols enjoys a lighthearted moment with San Francisco manager Dusty Baker during the 2002 NLCS. (opposite) Pujols hoists the jersey of fallen teammate Darryl Kile during the celebration of the Cardinals division championship. Kile had passed away before a game in Chicago and the team carried him with them in spirit for the rest of the season.

pitch, and he might hit a home run to right field. He's not concerned about pulling the ball."

The ability to make adjustments between at-bats helped Pujols become the first hitter since Ted Williams to drive in more than 250 runs in his first two seasons in the majors. He became the first Cardinal since Stan Musial in 1950–51 to finish in the top four in the MVP balloting in consecutive years.

For many young players, having their name linked with Hall of Fame legends such as Williams and Musial would have been intimidating, but Pujols had already proven that he was not a typical young player.

"I don't know why people say I'm not supposed to be doing what I'm doing," Pujols said. "I'm just trying to do my job. I'm blessed, and I'm glad I'm blessed."

Not many hitters, even veterans who have played in the majors for years, had the ability to correct a flaw or make a change in their hitting approach as easily as Pujols did. It was no doubt one of the secrets to his success.

"What makes him special is that things come naturally," said pitcher Tom Glavine. "It's no big overhaul in his swing to hit the ball with power the other way. You can't just work him away and hope for a single. You're just as fearful that he'll hit a home run to the opposite field."

As he prepared for his third year in the majors, Pujols was told by hitting coach Mitchell Page that pitchers would be varying the way they tried to work to him. How well Pujols adjusted to those changes would go a long way toward determining his future success, he said.

"When you can tell yourself what you are doing wrong and correct it the next at-bat, that's how you become a good hitter," Pujols said. "You don't want to do the same thing in three at-bats...then do something

different the last at-bat. By then it's too late.

"You want to make adjustments your first at-bat. You don't have to wait until somebody else corrects it. Sometimes it's better for people outside to say something, but 90 percent of the time I know what I'm doing wrong."

In the first half of the 2003 season, Pujols did very little wrong. He arrived at the All-Star Game in Chicago with a .368 average, 27 homers, and 86 RBIs—numbers that would have thrilled many players if they had put together those totals for an entire season.

Pujols had already established a reputation of being such a good hitter that even veterans with many more years of experience were coming to him, asking for advice. One player who did so was Cincinnati's Sean Casey, even though he had hit .332 in the majors in 1999 while Pujols was still in junior college.

"You talk to him about hitting, and you can't believe you're listening to a 23-year-old guy," Casey said. "He has such a good idea about it all—staying inside the ball, hitting in counts, covering the plate with two strikes, his approach.

"It's amazing how much he already knows, how much he's figured out."

One of the things Pujols had figured out was that it was his obligation to give back to the game, to be thankful for what the game had provided for him and his family, by sharing his knowledge of hitting with whoever asked.

It did not matter to Pujols whether the person seeking help was on his team or an opponent.

"If there's somebody on the other side who comes and asks me about hitting, I might tell him during the game, 'hey, you're jumping,'" Pujols said. "Sometimes I remember he's on the other side and I say, 'I'll tell you

Despite only being in his third major league season, Pujols already had the admiration and respect of the game's finest hitters. His prowess at the plate was the stuff of envy and even fellow All-Stars like Seattle's Ichiro Suzuki took notice.

tomorrow.' But I'm not a selfish player. I like to help out everybody. I want the best for my teammates, and I'm pretty sure they want the best for me."

It was easy for Pujols' teammates to root for him, and root they did.

"It's gotten to the point where you don't even marvel at it anymore," said veteran Tino Martinez. "You just kind of expect it. Yeah, you expect him to hit home runs. You expect him to drive in runs. You expect him to have great at-bats every time. We're just used to seeing it.

"I've played with great, great players, guys who put up some good numbers. But I've never seen a guy as focused as he is. The focus is unbelievable."

Opposing pitchers also were ready to put Pujols in a special class, reserved for the truly great players in the history of the game.

"I'm most impressed by his ability not to swing at balls out of the strike zone," said the Cubs' Kerry Wood.

"It's amazing to have such discipline at that age. With his ability, you take your chances and try to get him to chase a pitch. Usually he doesn't."

What Pujols was chasing in 2003 was his first batting championship. With the Cardinals out of the playoff race for the first time in his career, headed for a third-place finish, pursuing the batting title gave Pujols a focus for the latter part of the season.

Two hits in the final game of the year allowed him to withstand a furious charge by Todd Helton of the Rockies to win the batting title. Pujols' final average of .35871 was just ahead of Helton's .35849. It was the closest batting race in National League history and the third closest in major league history.

At age 23, Pujols became the youngest batting champ in the NL since the Dodgers' Tommy Davis won the title in 1962, when he also was 23.

The .359 average was the highest by a Cardinal since

(above) Pujols was a superstar from his rookie season, but he never displays superstar affectations on the field. He tries to help his team win and make his teammates better, something players and managers around the league respect. (opposite) No player hit better than Pujols in 2003. He held off a late charge by Colorado's Todd Helton to win the batting title with an impressive .359 average.

Pujols accepts the Silver Bat from Chuck Schuup of Hillerich & Bradsby early in 2004 in recognition of his National League batting title from the year before. He has never hit worse than .314 for a season in his career.

Joe Torre hit .363 in 1971. And it wasn't as if Pujols did not accomplish anything else that season except get base hits.

His overall totals—43 homers, 124 RBIs, 137 runs scored, 212 hits, 51 doubles—marked one of the best individual seasons in franchise history. Pujols led the major leagues in runs, doubles, extra-base hits, and total bases. The only other player in the Cardinals' more than 100-year history who had hit more than 40 homers and collected more than 200 hits in one season was Rogers Hornsby in 1922.

Pujols also recorded a 30-game hitting streak, matching Musial for the second longest streak in team history, three games shorter than Hornsby's streak in 1922. Pujols' chance of passing either of the Hall of Famers was stopped by a case of the flu, which sidelined him for four days. He went 0-for-5 when he returned to the lineup.

Having Pujols miss four games because of illness actually proved to more than a few pitchers that he

was human after all.

"As a player, you know if you make a mistake he is going to make you pay for it," said Florida pitcher Chad Fox. "But he can still find a way to produce with your best pitch. That's intimidating."

Pujols' 43 homers increased his career total to 114, matching Ralph Kiner's record for the most homers through a player's first three seasons. He joined Mark McGwire and Jose Canseco as the only players to hit 30 or more homers in each of their first three years. For the second consecutive year, Pujols finished second in MVP voting.

As more and more people tried to analyze what the secrets were to Pujols' success, Pujols himself admitted that he thought one of his best attributes was that he had quick hands.

"The key to hitting is the hands," he said. "You leave your hands back so even if you jump at the ball, your hands are back. If it's a breaking ball, you can still put a

(above) Two of the great offensive forces in baseball share some friendly words before an August 2003 game. Baseball's all-time home run leader, Barry Bonds, is on the list of baseballs' luminaries who admire Pujols' approach at the plate. (opposite) Despite being primarily a first baseman today, Pujols is a versatile defensive player, as as he shows while tracking down a ball at the wall while playing outfield in 2003.

good swing on it. Sometimes you're going to get fooled on a breaking ball. Then you adjust the next pitch. But what's most important is for my hands to be in the right position for me to drive the ball.

"If it's away, I can drive the ball away. If it's inside I can pull the ball down the line."

His individual success, however, did not mask Pujols' disappointment at the Cardinals failure to make the playoffs. He came to spring training in 2004 with only one goal in mind—winning the pennant and being able to play in the World Series.

The Cardinals had come close a couple of times in recent years, losing in the NLCS in 1996, 2000, and 2002, but had not played in the World Series since 1987 and had not won the world championship since 1982. For a franchise with as long and as rich a history as the Cardinals, that was a long drought.

The Cardinals had been impressed enough with

Pujols' performance in the first three years of his career that before the start of the 2004 campaign they rewarded him with the largest contract in franchise history—a seven year deal worth $100 million.

If Pujols felt he had been under pressure before, that feeling was only magnified as he began to work under the new contract. Whether it was the pressure or other factors, Pujols did not have a Pujols-like April, hitting only .287 with seven homers and 17 RBIs. It marked the first time he had failed to hit .300 for a month since June 2002.

The team also got off to a sluggish start and by the end of May was only four games over .500 at 27–23, but luckily they were still in second place in the NL Central. That was about to change.

Led by Pujols, the Cardinals won 27 of their final 37 games before the All-Star break, improving their record to 54–33 and opening up a seven-game lead in the division.

"The best thing about Albert is that he's playing to

(above) Yadier Molina made a perfect throw from behind home plate and Pujols expertly laid down the tag to pick off Pittsburgh's Rob Mackowiak in a 2004 contest. The Pirates swept the series, but it had little effect in slowing the Cardinals. (opposite) Son Albert Jr. joins his dad on the walk from the clubhouse to the practice field during spring training in 2004. The Cards got off to a sluggish start that year, but quickly found their groove in the National League Central.

win," said La Russa. "He's playing for a ring for himself, his teammates, and the Cardinal fans. That's what I admire about him most. Nothing else is a close second. The true winning player lets the numbers, the stats, and the money happen. That's what he does."

In July and August combined, Pujols hit 21 home runs and drove in 51 runs in 51 games, in the process surpassing both the 30- and 40-homer marks. In addition, he recorded the first three-homer game of his career, on July 20 at Wrigley Field against the Cubs. No other player in history had ever hit 30 or more home runs in each of his first four seasons.

"It's got to be pretty hard, really hard, if nobody's ever done it," La Russa said. "He's a smarter hitter (now). He's had three and a half great years. People are more aware of him. To maintain what you're doing, you've got to improve."

Pujols agreed with his manager that as impressive as those accomplishments were, he was more impressed with the team's success. By the end of August the Cardinals were 43 games over .500 at 87–44 and were sitting on a 15½-game lead over the second place team.

"I don't care what kind of numbers I put up or who they compare me to," Pujols said. "I just want to be a winner. When you start thinking about your numbers and what you've done in the big leagues, that's when you start feeling comfortable, and I don't want to do that."

Neither the Cardinals nor Pujols let up in September, even though the division title was a certainty, and the team finished with 105 victories—one short of the most in franchise history. His 46 homers were a career high; he drove in 123 runs and scored 133 times to go along with his .331 average.

No player in the history of the game had ever put together such numbers for the first four years of a career, but as the playoffs began, none of that mattered to

(above) Pujols scoops up a grounder while learning the nuances of playing first base. He broke into the majors playing third base, and also made a few starts at first base early in his career. An injury scare in 2003 permanently brought him in from the outfield. (opposite) A pumped-up Pujols celebrates with Scott Rolen in a win over the Cubs during his monumental summer. He hit three homers on this day and carried the Cardinals to an 11–8 win.

The individual recognition was great—no player had ever started a career like Pujols—but he was determined to lead the Cardinals to the pinnacle of sports in October 2004.

Pujols. His mind was focused on a different number—11—the number of playoff wins a team needs to win the World Series.

The Cardinals' first-round opponent was the Dodgers, and Pujols immediately set the tone with a home run in the bottom of the first inning. A pair of 8–3 victories gave the Cardinals a commanding two-games-to-none lead as the series moved to Los Angeles. Jose

Lima's shutout in game three gave the Dodgers a little life, but Pujols took care of that in the fourth game.

With the score tied 2–2, Pujols came up in the fourth inning and blasted a three-run homer that sent the Cardinals on to a 6–2 win and another berth in the National League Championship Series.

Waiting for them were the Houston Astros, who had developed into the Cardinals' biggest rival of the decade.

(above) There was no slow start to the 2004 NLCS for Pujols, who socked a homer in his first at-bat of the series to put the Cardinals in front. (opposite) Pujols points into the dugout after his eighth inning homer in Game 2 of the 2004 NLCS, breaking open a tie game. When Scott Rolen followed with a homer of his own, the Cardinals were on their way to a 2–0 series lead.

Pujols made certain this series began the same way as the division series, slamming a two-run homer in the first inning that launched the Cardinals to a 10–7 victory.

Pujols again came through in the second game, hitting another homer, this time in the eighth inning, to break a 4–4 tie. When Scott Rolen followed with another homer, it marked the first time in franchise history that players had hit back-to-back homers in a postseason game.

The Cardinals now had a two-games-to-none lead as the series shifted to Houston, and Pujols and his teammates knew two more wins would give them the pennant and the World Series berth. They also knew winning in Houston would not be easy—the Astros had lost only one home game since August 22.

They didn't lose now, either. Despite another Pujols homer in game four, the Astros won all three games at home and brought a three-games-to-two edge back to Busch Stadium.

For the first time all season, the Cardinals faced elimination in Game 6, and the Astros took a 1–0 lead in the top of the first. Pujols came to bat in the bottom of the inning with one runner on, and he slammed his sixth homer of the postseason to put the Cardinals ahead 2–1. His leadoff double in the third sparked a two-run inning that increased the lead to 4–2, but the St. Louis bullpen could not hold the lead, and the game went into extra innings with the score tied at 4.

In the 12th, Pujols drew a leadoff walk and then trotted home on Jim Edmonds' two-run walkoff homer, setting up a seventh and deciding game.

All Pujols knew was that they now once again controlled their own destiny…win the seventh game and they were in the World Series.

"We don't want to wait until next year," he said. "One hundred and sixty-two games and wait and see if we're going to be in this situation. There's one game away to get us to the next level. We're going to try to make it happen."

Pujols knew the task would not be easy. Starting the game for the Astros was Roger Clemens, one of the best pitchers in the history of the game. La Russa, for one, was betting on Pujols to come through.

"He's playing like a man possessed because he wants to win a league championship and go to the next level," La Russa said. "He's got a bunch of teammates who are playing the same way. He's into it."

To Pujols, it did not matter if he turned out to be the hero or if it was one of his teammates. All he wanted was to be on the winning team.

"If one guy fails, then the other guy knows he has to pick it up," Pujols said. "That's why we've been so successful."

The Astros gave Clemens a 2–1 lead going into the bottom of the sixth inning, and Pujols came to bat with the tying run on third. Pujols was only two for 14 in his career against Clemens and was hitless in five at-bats against him in this series, compared to a 12-for-21 performance against the rest of the Houston staff. Even with first base open, the Astros decided to pitch to him.

On a 1-2 pitch, Clemens left a fastball up, and Pujols pounced on it for a double to left field, scoring the tying run. On the next pitch, Pujols trotted home on a two-run blast by Scott Rolen that gave the Cardinals a 4–2 lead.

The Cardinals were now just nine outs away from the win, and when the St. Louis relievers closed out a 5–2 triumph, Pujols and his teammates found themselves celebrating.

Cardinals players swarm the plate as Jim Edmonds touches home following his game-winning blast. Pujols had walked to lead off the inning and scored the winning run.

"This is what you dream about, going to the World Series, as a little boy,"said Pujols, who was named the MVP of the series. "Everyone in this locker room is the MVP. That's why the trophy will be staying in the locker room for the rest of my career."

After the celebration, the Cardinals realized they had precious little time to get ready for their opponent in the World Series, the Boston Red Sox. The Cardinals had only one day off between their Game 7 win and the opening game of the series, in Boston.

Whether that short turnaround was the reason or not, the Cardinals did not play well in the series and were swept by the Red Sox, who won their first world championship since 1918.

Pujols was 5-for-15 but was held without a home run or an RBI. The Cardinals hit just .199 as a team.

"It seemed like everything was going their way," Pujols said. "But we had a great year. I'm proud of the way we battled. It didn't finish like we wanted; it just didn't happen."

If he needed any additional motivation going into his next season, losing the World Series provided it for Pujols. Coming so close to his goal, and falling short, left Pujols even more determined to make that goal a reality. ∎

(above) Jim Edmonds did the heavy lifting in the deciding moment of Game 6, knocking the walk-off homer that sent the NLCS to a climactic Game 7. (opposite) Unfortunately, the Cardinals run to the World Series ended in disappointment. The Red Sox were able to break the "Curse of the Bambino," and the Cards were left wondering what might have been.

Pujols fires home to force Boston's Bill Mueller at the plate in Game 1 of the 2004 World Series. With only one day of rest between the NLCS and Game 1, the Cardinals were fairly well spent by the time the Series began.

MVP and a World Champion

By the start of the 2005 season, the question being asked around baseball was not about what Pujols had accomplished in his first four major league seasons. That performance was unprecedented.

The question was about the future and how good Pujols could be. Could he possibly continue his performance for years to come, or maybe, put up even better numbers?

All of that talk bothered Pujols, who knew from his failed World Series experience that his only goal remained to win the fall classic.

"All I want to do is win some championships," Pujols said. "I want to take advantage of every single opportunity that comes my way. I got a taste of the World Series last year. It didn't turn out the way we wanted, but that's part of the game. Hopefully we'll get that taste again this year. It doesn't come in a package. You have to put yourself together and work hard for it."

That was the advice he gave whenever he was asked to speak to younger players. Texas Tech basketball coach Bob Knight, a close friend of La Russa, asked Pujols to address his team when they traveled to Columbia, Missouri, to play the Missouri Tigers over the winter. He also spoke to the Cardinals' minor league players during spring training.

"I want to help those kids out," Pujols said. "I love the game. You play for little kids and hopefully to make a good name for yourself. It's not about getting credit. My name is out there for things I've done in the past. It's not like I need credit. I just want to help those guys out. It's what's in me. Nobody can keep me from doing that. I'm going to do it until I'm done playing."

Pujols is particularly generous not only with his time but with donations of equipment and other necessities to young Latin players.

"I lived that," he said. "I was there once, and I know what it takes. I know what it is and how tough it is to come here knowing no English. Anything they need I'll try to make it available to them. You just need to encourage them to keep working hard and take advantage of the opportunities they get."

Pujols knows what it would have meant for him, as a young player, to receive that attention from a major league star.

With a new drive to win a championship after reaching baseball's biggest stage in 2004, Pujols began 2005 on a tear that did not stop until the season ended and he was crowned the National League MVP. Here, he looks to take an extra base as Philadelphia's Jimmy Rollins chases an errant throw.

80

Pujols settles into his familiar defensive squat, ready to pounce against the Pittsburgh Pirates in August 2009.

"Hopefully they'll look at me and say, 'I want to be like Albert Pujols,'" he said. "It's always good when people can look at you and say 'I want to be like him' because that means they can learn things on the field and off the field."

When the younger players were watching Pujols on the field, most observers now believed they were watching the best player in the game. Larry Walker, acquired by the Cardinals from Colorado in 2004, admitted what every player in the majors knew to be true.

"Anytime we faced him or Vlad (Vladimir Guerrero) we referred to them as the freaks," Walker said. "I'm to the point now where when we're on the bench, we just look at each other and give a little smirk and a laugh."

Part of the reason for his success, however, was that Pujols still was trying to improve. He knew he needed to do better if the Cardinals were going to win the World Series.

"He's never satisfied," said Cardinals reliever Jason Isringhausen. "A lot of guys who can hit don't give a flip about defense. He moved to first base last year, and he's already one of the best guys in the league there. It's not amazing just because of how good he is; it's amazing because he always wants to get better."

Led by Pujols, the Cardinals moved into first place in the NL Central before the 2005 season was two weeks old and stayed there the rest of the season, building a lead as large as 16 games over the second-place team.

Some players, given that large cushion, would naturally relax and begin coasting en route to the playoffs but not Pujols.

At the All-Star break, he once again was displaying his consistency—a .337 average with 22 homers and 69 RBIs. He followed up the first half with a strong finish, hitting .320 after the break, with 19 homers and 48 RBIs.

The totals left him with a .330 average for the season, with 41 homers and 117 RBIs. He finished second in the NL in average, third in homers, and tied for second in RBIs. He led the NL with 129 runs scored.

When Pujols surpassed 100 RBIs for the fifth consecutive season, La Russa knew how memorable a moment it was. The only players who had ever driven in 100 or

(above) Pujols delivered phenomenal consistency in 2005, but it was his teammates who were also responsible for bringing him home a league-best 129 times. (opposite) Pushing ever harder to win a championship, Pujols led his team with a fiery attitude. After getting caught stealing in this 2005 game, Pujols was ejected for arguing with the umpire.

more runs their first five seasons were all Hall of Famers...Al Simmons, Ted Williams, and Joe DiMaggio.

"When you're talking about the best first five years in major league history, how's that not huge?" La Russa asked. "It's historic. We're not going to be cool about that one. We just saw history. I don't think you see history in this game that often. When you see it, you applaud it."

Pujols and the Cardinals hoped the applause continued well into October. Their first-round opponent in the playoffs was the San Diego Padres, who quickly disappeared from the scene, being swept by St. Louis in three straight games.

For the second consecutive year, that set up an NLCS matchup between the Cardinals and the Houston Astros, who finished 11 games behind St. Louis in the regular season but beat Atlanta in their first-round matchup.

There was no reason to expect this series to be any different than the matchup had been the previous year, one of the most dramatic postseason series in the Cardinals' history. The teams split the first two games, in St. Louis, meaning the Cardinals traveled to Houston knowing they had to win at least one game there if they wanted to get the series back to St. Louis.

Their chances did not look good after Houston posted 4–3 and 2–1 victories in the third and fourth games and built a 4–2 lead heading into the ninth inning of Game 5. The Astros, who had never played in a World Series, had their locker room covered in plastic and were uncorking the champagne bottles in preparation for their celebration as Brad Lidge took the mound to begin the inning.

He retired the first two batters. The NL championship trophy was wheeled into the Astros' clubhouse. In

(above) Heading home after one of his 41 round-trippers in 2005, Pujols carried his team into the playoffs and was looking for redemption from the year before. (opposite) Scoring thanks to a Ronnie Belliard single, Pujols slides home in front of Astros catcher Brad Ausmus. This September matchup was important and turned out to be a preview of the National League playoffs.

center field, workers were ready to drop a large "2005 National League Champions" banner. Fans in the stands were on their feet, clapping and yelling.

Lidge worked the count on David Eckstein to 1–2. The Astros were one strike away. Eckstein, at least for the moment, delayed the celebration with a single. Jim Edmonds came up and worked Lidge for a walk. The tying runs were now on base. The fans temporarily stopped their cheers.

Pujols came to the plate. This was the kind of special moment he had prepared for, the challenge that all great players want—to be at the plate, game on the line, and in this case, the pennant on the line.

On Lidge's second pitch, a hanging slider, Pujols unleashed one of the most dramatic homers in Cardinals' history. The bomb hit the train tracks well above and beyond the left field fence for a three-run homer. Instead of going home as a disappointed loser, Pujols' homer had sent the series back to St. Louis for a sixth game. Never has a stadium gone from a frenzied roar to a funeral-like stillness so quickly. Said Pujols, "It was like pressing the mute button on the TV."

It was several hours later, about 4:00 AM, when Pujols walked into his St. Louis home. His young son, A.J., greeted him at the door.

"I love you Dad," he said. "Glad you're home. Nice home run."

The city of St. Louis could not have said it any better.

The momentous home run, of course, really accomplished only one goal—it kept the Cardinals alive. The true importance of the blast would only be measured by whether the Cardinals were able to come home and win the final two games and win the series.

Unfortunately for Pujols and the Cardinals, that was not meant to be. The Astros rode the strong performance of Roy Oswalt to a 5–1 win in Game 6, the final game at Busch Stadium, which was torn down after the season to make way for a new ballpark just south of the stadium that had stood since 1966.

That stadium had witnessed plenty of great moments and players over the years, and certainly the latest star, Pujols, had already earned his place among the Cardinals' elite. There was still an empty spot on his mantel, however, reserved for a Most Valuable Player award.

The award that had eluded him, despite four outstanding seasons, was finally his when he received 18 of 32 first-place votes by members of the Baseball Writers Association of America. Pujols received a total of 378 points, defeating runnerup Andruw Jones of the Braves by 27 points.

"When I got that call, it felt almost like that home run I hit against Brad Lidge," Pujols said. "Everyone was calling saying how much I deserved that. It's a great feeling. But you still need to be humble. You can't let this award take you too high."

Pujols won the award despite the fact that he did not have the best year of his career either in batting average, homers, or RBIs.

"I don't think it was my best year," he said. "It wasn't the best year for us because we didn't win the championship. We didn't even make it to the World Series. So I don't think it was the best year. Of course I'd take 40 home runs, .300, and 100-some RBIs every year. That's not my goal, but I'd take it every year."

His ultimate goal, of course, was still to become a World Series champion, a goal he hoped would come true in 2006.

Astros reliever Brad Lidge can only watch as Pujols' game-winning three-run homer sails off into the night in the 2005 NLCS. The Astros won the next game and advanced to the World Series.

In a column in the *St. Louis Post-Dispatch* on April 4, 2006, Bernie Miklasz wrote, "If you thought the MVP award was going to make Albert Pujols complacent, make his head swell...stand back, and clear out, because he might just take that thick MVP plaque and smack you upside your head for suggesting such foolishness."

Miklasz's column came after Pujols opened the 2006 season with a two-homer game at Philadelphia.

"I'm always going to be hungry for that ring," Pujols said. "And when I get that first one, I want another one. Because winning never gets old. I just thank God that he has blessed me with great teammates and a great team. That's my goal, to make sure I concentrate on that ring. I've got a lot accomplished. I got an MVP last year. But that's in the past. If I can trade up for a World Series ring, I would love to do that. Because that's what it's all about: the ring."

That is exactly why La Russa is so fond of Pujols: his attitude and the desire to spread it to everyone in the Cardinals' clubhouse.

"He is totally dedicated to winning the game," La Russa said. "There isn't anything else that's even close. Everything else is a distant second. He's just trying to win the game.

"Albert really wants it, and he's working so hard to make it happen. The day this man gets that big World Series ring, it will be a really, really special day. Here's a guy through all the distractions of modern-day baseball has refused to give in to them. And for that, I admire him the most."

La Russa has been involved in baseball long enough to know that sometimes the difference between winning and losing can be very small, and the players, such as Pujols, who pay attention to even the smallest detail are usually the ones who are the most successful.

So it came as no real surprise that before the new Busch Stadium was three weeks old, Pujols discovered a

(above) Pujols can't help but peek over the shoulder of Fred Hanser—part of the Cardinals ownership group—as he reads a statement from manager Tony La Russa at Pujols' 2005 MVP press conference. **(opposite)** Pujols smiles with his three-year-old son Albert Jr. as they sit at the press conference announcing big Albert as the 2005 National League MVP. It was not his best statistical season, but he still won comfortably over challengers Andruw Jones and Derrek Lee.

"He is totally dedicated to winning the game. There isn't anything that's even close. Everything else is a distant second."

—Tony La Russa on Albert Pujols

flaw that he thought needed correcting.

After playing three night games at the stadium, Pujols told teammates and stadium officials that he had trouble seeing in the batter's box late in the games.

So he went out and stood at home plate while stadium workers readjusted the angle of the lights, until Pujols reported the problem solved.

Unfortunately for NL pitchers, they had no way to solve the problem of how to try to pitch to Pujols, no matter what they tried.

Pujols enjoyed the best April of his career in 2006, hitting .346 with 14 homers and 32 RBIs. The 14 homers established a major league record for April, topping the old record of 13 that had been set by Ken Griffey Jr. and Luis Gonzalez. His 32 RBIs tied the team record for April, set by McGwire in 1998.

More important to Pujols, of course, was that his performance helped the Cardinals set a franchise record with 17 wins in April.

"The best way to deal with him is to make sure the two guys in front of him have the most miserable nights in their offensive careers," said Jim Tracy, then the manager of the Pirates. "It's very easy to say just to walk this guy, but is that also to say that 100 percent of the time you can get Scott Rolen out?"

The Cubs' Ryan Dempster was one of the unlucky pitchers who had to try to come up with a game plan on how to attack Pujols.

"You've got to be aggressive," Dempster said. "It doesn't matter if it's 0−2 or 2−0. I still believe if you execute your pitch, you can get a guy out. When he's hot like he is now, there's not really a lot of space to do your executing...maybe a postage stamp."

A fellow pitcher who felt the same way was the Pirates' Ian Snell, who basically admitted that the only thing to do with Pujols was to hope for the best, then tip your hat.

After giving up one particularly long homer to Pujols, Snell said, "I hung it, and he banged it. I thought it was going to hit the Arch. I wanted to go high-five him. That's unreal. That's like Superman playing baseball."

Pujols carried his hot April into May, hitting 11 homers and driving in 33 runs, even though his average for the month "slumped" to .289.

One pitcher who was glad he did not have to worry about Pujols was Chris Carpenter, one of his teammates on the Cardinals. He marveled at how well Pujols handled all of the pressure he faced every game.

"That's a lot of pressure to put on one guy to expect him every time he comes up there to do something huge," Carpenter said. "Guys in the media and fans...if he gets a base hit and drives in two runs, it's like they say, 'That's sweet, he got a base hit and drove in two runs.' But everybody in the stands is like, 'I wish he had hit a homer.'"

Naturally, about the only person not impressed with Pujols' performance was Pujols himself.

"I know I have a chance to get better," he said. "How can I start? How can I finish? I don't try to do too much. I try to help the team win games. If they want to pitch around me, we have the guys surrounding me who can do damage."

One of the ways Pujols did think he could improve was actually trying to take more pitches and accept walks. That would make him a more patient hitter, he said, and assure that he was swinging only at pitches that he had a chance to hit.

His competitive spirit burning brighter than ever, Pujols dedicated himself to making 2006 the year the Cardinals won the World Series. Here, San Diego's Josh Barfield and Terrmel Sledge wind up at the same base after being hounded by Pujols in a rundown.

"It's definitely going to make you better because it's going to make you more disciplined and more relaxed," Pujols said. "You know if it's not in that spot, you won't hit it."

About the only way to slow Pujols down, everyone knew, was an injury. One scout actually turned in his advance report on the Cardinals and said of Pujols, "Hope he gets hit in the ankle the series before you see him."

It was not an ankle but a strained right oblique muscle that sent him to the disabled list on June 4 for the first time in his career. At the time Pujols led the majors with 25 homers and 65 RBIs. Doctors told Pujols he would likely be sidelined from four to six weeks. In true Pujols fashion, he missed only 15 games.

The Cardinals were in first place when Pujols went out, were still there when he returned, and by mid-September had a built a seven-game lead as they appeared on their way to the playoffs for the third consecutive year.

A seven-game losing streak, however, wiped out almost all of that lead, and the Cardinals were only four outs away from suffering an eighth consecutive loss, against the Padres on September 27, when Pujols came to bat with two runners on base. He turned on a fastball from Cla Meredith and delivered a three-run, perhaps pennant-saving, homer.

"I might make that pitch 100 times a year and get away with it," said Meredith, who had a 0.72 ERA. "Not tonight. He's Albert Pujols. What more can you say?"

The blast was Pujols' career-high 47th homer, and none was more important. Victories in two of the final four games of the year left the Cardinals with just 83 wins, but that was good enough to win the NL Central by 1½ games and earn another spot in the postseason.

Pujols had been involved in enough playoff games to know that what happened in the regular season meant nothing once your team became one of the

(above) Pujols accepts a commemorative shadow box in 2006 in recognition of his record-breaking April. The hardware was nice recognition for the player, but he was focused on team success. (opposite) Pujols walks to the dugout after striking out against the Chicago Cubs. He left the game one inning later with a muscle strain that put him on the 15-day disabled list.

Pujols sits in the dugout during the ninth inning in a game against the San Francisco Giants on June 30, 2009, in St. Louis. Pujols hit two home runs but the Giants won, 6–3.

eight still playing in October.

"Everything seemed like it was going the opposite way," Pujols said about the Cardinals' end-of-season struggles. "Hopefully this week it clicks our way. This is a good time to get hot."

The best chance the Cardinals had of winning, of course, was if Pujols got hot. The best way for opponents to win, including first-round foe San Diego, was to figure out how to slow down, if not shut down, Pujols.

According to scouts whose job it was to prepare their teams on how to face opponents, that was an almost impossible task. Previewing the St. Louis—San Diego matchup, scout John Stockstill of the Cubs told the *Washington Post,* "You might as well throw the report in the garbage. Pujols is one of those rare guys that there is no way to pitch to him. He's the type of hitter that gets himself out before a pitcher will get him out."

Pujols' homer off Jake Peavy in the opening game once again set the tone for the series, and the Cardinals won in four games, moving on to face the New York Mets for the NL pennant. When the Cardinals and Mets split the first four games, it was down to a best-of-three show-down. Pujols had not played well in the early part of the series and also had appeared moody and grumpy, especially with the New York press corps.

One of the reasons, he finally explained to *St. Louis Post-Dispatch* columnist Bryan Burwell, was that a beloved uncle, who had helped to raise him, had died the previous week from a heart attack. "This should be fun," Pujols said. "It hasn't been, because I lost my uncle. You know how tough it is when someone you love dies? That's what I've been going through."

Pujols also finally admitted that he was feeling some internal pressure because he wanted so badly to win a World Series.

"I care about this so much," he told Burwell. "I know the people in St. Louis are expecting a lot out of us because they want to win a World Series as much as I do. I feel the pressure to deliver that World Series that they haven't had in a long time."

In the fifth game, Pujols finally was able to smile. His first home run of the series helped St. Louis to a 4–2 victory, and the Cardinals packed for New York knowing they were one win away from the World Series. The Mets did not quit, however, and forced a seventh and deciding game with a 4–2 win in Game 6.

The seventh game was one of the most pressurized contests in recent postseason history. The Cardinals and Mets were tied at 1 going into the ninth inning, thanks to New York left fielder Endy Chavez' home-run saving catch of a shot hit by Scott Rolen in the sixth.

Chavez could not reach a two-run bomb hit by Yadier Molina in the ninth however, and when Adam Wainwright froze Carlos Beltran on perhaps the best curve ball of his career in the bottom of the inning, the Cardinals were once again NL champions and were headed to Detroit to play the Tigers.

Given another chance, Pujols and his teammates were determined not to suffer the same misfortune that hit them in 2004, being swept by the Red Sox. He once again homered in the first game of this series, off Justin Verlander, to help the Cardinals win 7–2.

The Tigers won Game 2 behind veteran Kenny Rogers, but the Cardinals came home confident that they were playing well enough to win. And win they did, claiming all three games in St. Louis to close out the 10th world

The thrill of victory and the agony of defeat: Albert Pujols runs in to celebrate with teammates after the last out of the 2006 NLCS, while New York's Endy Chavez dejectedly jogs off the field.

championship in franchise history.

Even though Pujols was only a combined 2-for-9 in those three games, and hit just .200 for the series, neither he, the rest of the Cardinals, or their fans cared—the team, despite having won the fewest games in the regular season since 1999, was the World Champions. Pujols had finally earned his ring.

In a chaotic Cardinals clubhouse, Pujols grabbed a bottle of champagne and with his wife, Deidre, snuck under the plastic protecting the players' lockers. The couple hugged, and then Pujols emerged to join the celebration.

"This is what you play for; this means everything to me," Pujols said. "More than anything in my house; more than all the trophies and awards. This is my dream. I want to cry. It doesn't matter what kind of numbers you put up. It doesn't matter how much money you make. If you don't have a ring, you don't have everything. You're not a winner."

Pujols also had to clear a space on his mantel for another award, his first Gold Glove. That, and the satisfaction of winning the World Series, offset another second-place finish, Pujols' third, in the league MVP vote. Despite finishing third in the league in average, second in homers, and second in RBIs—despite missing two weeks—he was edged out by the Phillies' Ryan Howard for the MVP honor.

Despite now having won virtually every honor it was possible to win in the game, Pujols still was not satisfied with what he had accomplished. His goal was set high.

"I want to be the best player that ever plays baseball," Pujols said. "Is that going to happen? I don't know. I don't read the future. God only reads the future. I want to be in the Hall of Fame. I want to do that." ■

(above) Scott Rolen and Pujols high five teammates after coming home on Jim Edmonds' double in Game 3 of the World Series. (opposite) The celebration begins as the Cardinals are crowned World Champions. Pujols hugs third baseman Scott Rolen, on whose face the thrill of victory is clearly etched.

Chasing the Triple Crown

The question is not *whether* Albert Pujols can win the Triple Crown, the question is *will* he win it?

No hitter has led his league in the three most important batting categories—average, home runs, and RBIs—since Carl Yastrzemski did it for the Boston Red Sox in 1967. The wait in the National League has been even longer, since Joe Medwick of the Cardinals did it in 1937.

Not only has a hitter not led in all three categories since then, no one really has come close. The closest, perhaps, was Stan Musial of the Cardinals in 1948, who led the NL in average and RBIs but hit only 39 home runs, one less than league leaders Ralph Kiner and Johnny Mize.

Alex Rodriguez, Manny Ramirez, and Barry Bonds have led all three categories, but never in the same season. The last hitter to be leading in all three at the All-Star break was Hank Aaron. Rodriguez and Ryan Howard are the only active players who have led two of the three categories in the same season, home runs and RBIs, but were never in contention for the batting title in those years.

Pujols has shown he could do it by actually leading the NL in all three categories from the All-Star break in 2008 through the All-Star break in 2009, hitting .347, with 51 homers and 153 RBIs.

"You just don't see that combination anymore," said Twins catcher Joe Mauer. "You usually have a guy who hits home runs who will hit .220 or .230. A high average guy might hit 10 or 15 home runs. But he (Pujols) puts it all together."

Said Brewers' outfielder Ryan Braun, "If anybody can do it, he can. I just marvel at his consistency. He gets pitched to the way Barry Bonds was pitched to. He gets one pitch per at-bat or one pitch every other at-bat, and he finds a way to center it up, which is incredible. He finds a way to get the barrel (of the bat) to the ball more consistently than anybody else in baseball. He's an amazing player, he really is."

Only 12 players have won the Triple Crown, and Rogers Hornsby and Ted Williams are the only players to do it twice. It actually happened fairly frequently in the early part of the 1900s. In the 25 years between 1922 and 1947, it happened eight times. The only players to win it since 1947 are

Mickey Mantle in 1956, Frank Robinson in 1966, and Yastrzemski in 1967.

When Medwick became the last NL player to do it in 1937, it really was not regarded by the media as that big of a story.

The *St. Louis Globe-Democrat* did record the fact that Medwick had finished on top of all three categories, in the fifth paragraph of its game story, but did not refer to him winning the Triple Crown. The newspaper was more concerned with other details of a 6–4 loss to the Cubs at Wrigley Field that attracted only 8,451 fans.

Medwick finished the season with only one hit in his last nine at-bats and did not hit a home run in his final four games of the year, hitting only three in September. That was still good enough to raise his season total to 31, tying Mel Ott of the New York Giants for the title. Ott hit five home runs between August 27 and September 2 but then hit only one more the rest of the season and none in his final 21 games.

Medwick set a Cardinals' team record of 154 RBIs, which still stands, to win that title by 39 RBIs, and his batting average of .374 was good enough to win the title by 10 percentage points.

In contrast to Medwick's winning the Triple Crown despite a slow finish to the season, the last Triple Crown winner, Yastrzemski, had to go on a tear in September to win. He was a combined 7-for-8 in the final two games of the season, with a home run and six RBIs. In the last 10 games of the season he was 20-of-37, with four homers and 14 RBIs, raising his average from .312 to .326. He won the average crown by 15 percentage points, the RBI title by eight, and tied Harmon Killebrew for the home run title with 44.

Former player and current broadcaster Joe Morgan believes it is harder to win the Triple Crown now than it was in different eras.

"You can control your average and your home runs," Morgan said, "you don't have control over your RBIs. You have a lot of guys now who are capable of putting up numbers that are as big as Yastrzemski. And the more players who are capable of doing that, the harder it's going to be."

Except when they are playing him, other players are rooting for Pujols to add the title of Triple Crown winner to his resume.

"The guy is so much better than anybody else in baseball right now," said the Yankees' Mark Teixeira. "I'm rooting for him to win the Triple Crown because I want to be able to say that I played with a Triple Crown winner."

Added Los Angeles' Orlando Hudson, "His chances for the Triple Crown in the next 10 years are good. That dude is unbelievable. Every time he comes up I say, 'Where's he gonna hit it out this time?' All I can say is, 'Wow.'" ∎

The Best Player in the Game

With everything that Pujols had achieved in the first six years of his career, what was perhaps even more impressive was the work that Pujols the man, not the baseball player, had accomplished.

He and his wife, Deidre, established the Pujols Family Foundation in 2005 to help raise money and assist families with Down syndrome children and also to benefit children and programs in his native Dominican Republic. Even before creating his own foundation, Pujols already was helping a variety of charities.

There was the charity auction in which he bid $2,500 for the glove Roger Clemens wore during his 300th career victory, only to give the glove to a teenager with Down syndrome. At the annual Baseball Writers dinner in St. Louis, he bid $5,000 for an autographed Chris Carpenter jersey, five times the next highest bidder, and then gave it to the person he outbid. At another auction to benefit children with Down syndrome, he paid $3,000 each for two Florida vacation packages, then gave them away to kids at the dinner.

Every year, on Down Syndrome Awareness Day at Busch Stadium, Pujols is an active participant in the "Buddy Walk." Almost every year, one of the children involved asks Pujols to hit a home run for them during the game.

In 2002, he hit a home run and drove in three runs. The following year, his home run was a game-winning walkoff blast in the 13th inning. In 2006, he celebrated the day with the third three-homer game of his career.

"He always has extra inspiration on a day like today," La Russa said afterward. "He's amazing. He's better than ever on days like this."

Pujols admitted that he did not believe all of the home runs were a coincidence.

"It's always good to do something special for these kids," he said. "Once in a while the kids will say, 'Hit a home run for me.' It's a special day for those kids, me, my daughter, my family."

After sitting out the Buddy Walk game in 2007 because of a sore leg and elbow, Pujols was back in the lineup for the 2008 game and drilled another homer in his first at-bat, giving him six homers on eight of those special days.

"He's the one guy I know who can tell a kid

Pujols acknowledges the fans as he receives his Most Valuable Player Award for the 2008 season before a game against the Kansas City Royals on May 22, 2009 in St. Louis.

he'll ht two homers for you, and you know he's good for it, and then he does it," said pitcher Adam Wainwright.

Of course, Pujols' charity work involved more than just giving those kids a special thrill on one day a year. In January 2007, Pujols missed the Cardinals' trip to the White House, where President George W. Bush congratulated them on winning the World Series, because he was in the Dominican Republic, along with doctors and dentists from the St. Louis area, treating children who otherwise might not receive medical care.

"We went down there to work, and that's what we did," Pujols said. "Five days, 1,000 kids. The doctors deserve all of the credit. They did an unbelievable job. It was an experience for me and for them."

Another memorable experience, one Pujols considered one of the most important days of his life, came on February 7, 2007, when he became a United States citizen. It was the culmination of a nearly year-long process,

resulting in perfect scores on both oral and written exams and the completion of a successful background check.

"The United States opened the door for my family," Pujols told reporters. "It (the tests) was a lot of hard work, but I came through. They talked about everything... probably things you guys wouldn't be able to answer."

As he reported to spring training...as a U.S. citizen, an MVP, a Gold Glove winner, a batting champion, and a World Series champion...Pujols was not ready to look back. He was still looking forward.

"You can't be satisfied with the years you've had," he said. "If I hit 49 home runs last season, I want to hit 50 this year. If I hit .330, then I want to hit .331. I'm not saying I'll do it, but it's how I want to get better. That tells me instead of going back, I'm going to move forward."

Despite those intentions, Pujols got off to the worst start of his career in 2007, hitting just .250 in April. He warmed up as the summer arrived, but he still did not hit

(opposite) A man of real convictions, Pujols does not just pay lip service or write a check to help others. His care for children is well documented, and he serves as the honorary chairman of the Cardinals annual event where they let kids with Down syndrome walk the bases and take the field. (above) Pujols and his wife, Deidre, sit at a 2005 press conference announcing the creation of the Pujols Family Foundation. The foundation helps raise money for Down syndrome charities and also works for the impoverished and orphaned in the Dominican Republic.

a home run in the Cardinals' last 23 games prior to the All-Star break. His batting average did not reach the .300 mark until June. It was no coincidence that the team arrived at the break five games under .500.

The break did not even provide relief as Pujols' own manager did not play him in the All-Star Game, despite having a perfect opportunity to use him as a pinch-hitter in the bottom of the ninth inning. The NL trailed by a run, there were two outs, and the bases were loaded.

Instead, Aaron Rowand remained in the game and popped out for the final out.

La Russa's decision not to play Pujols in the game sparked a mini media controversy that there was a rift in the manager-player relationship, but both insisted that it was a nonstory and a nonissue.

"People want to start World War III with me and Tony, and I think they are picking the wrong person because I have got so much respect for Tony, and he has

so much respect for me," Pujols said.

Said La Russa, "I've been real clear about how I feel about Albert," noting that he had called him the best player he had ever managed, better than Carlton Fisk, Rickey Henderson, Jose Canseco, or Mark McGwire. "Nothing ever changes about that. Nothing ever will. Our relationship will stand the test of time. There wasn't a problem. There isn't a problem."

There were problems, however, with the Cardinals in the second half of 2007. The team did not play any better than it had before the All-Star break and finished the season six games under .500, the first time in Pujols' career he had been on a team with a losing record.

He hit a career-low 32 homers and drove in "just" 103 runs, also the fewest of his career, while hitting .327. For the first time in his career Pujols failed to score 100 runs, falling one short of that mark. For the first time in his career he did not finish among the top four players in

(opposite) Two players who will one day be looked at as among the best to ever play the game chat for a moment in 2007. The Reds Ken Griffey Jr. takes a cautious lead off of first base while Pujols holds him to the bag. **(above)** In 2008 the Cardinals won seven more games than in 2007, but they still finished fourth in the NL Central. The increased win total was due in part to Pujols, who won the MVP, and Rick Ankiel, who completed his incredible road back to the majors with a breakout season.

the league MVP voting, dropping to ninth.

Pujols entered 2008 vowing to himself not to let a season like that happen again, and he didn't.

"I guess the best thing that happened last year was I struggled for the first two months because I was taking too aggressive an approach," Pujols said early in the 2008 season. "Coming after the World Series, I tried to put too much weight on my shoulders.

"I learned from my mistakes. If they give me a good pitch to hit, I'm going to take advantage of it. But I may see only one good pitch an at-bat or one good pitch a night."

Opposing pitchers and managers, of course, had realized by now that they were better off walking Pujols, intentionally or unintentionally, than letting him beat them with a home run. A poll of all 30 managers by ESPN.com about which hitter they would least want to

pitch to with a game on the line was won easily by Pujols, who received 11 votes. Tied for second were Vladimir Guerrero and Alex Rodriguez, with four votes each.

Pujols hit .368 through May, with 14 homers and 37 RBIs, when he suffered an injury to his left calf and had to go on the disabled list for the second time in his career. After being sidelined for two weeks, he went 4-for-4 in his first game back in the lineup.

On July 4, Pujols celebrated with his 300th career home run, and he continued to blister pitchers after the All-Star break, hitting .366 in the second half of the season. His final average of .357 was the second best of his career. He ended up losing the batting title to Atlanta's Chipper Jones by seven percentage points.

He continued his streak of hitting at least 30 homers (37) and driving in 100 or more runs (116) and once again

(opposite) Pujols reacts after crushing a grand slam against the Reds on July 3, 2009, in Cincinnati. (above) Pujols smiles as the rain starts to fall in the ninth inning against the Washington Nationals on May 26, 2007.

scored an even 100 runs. He also surpassed 100 walks (104) for the first time in his career while striking out only 54 times in 524 at-bats.

There was no question it was an MVP-caliber season, but the question was whether voters would give him the award or not because of the Cardinals' fourth-place finish in the NL Central, even though they won eight more games than in 2007.

His biggest competition was once again the Phillies' Ryan Howard, who led the NL in homers and RBIs and led the Phillies to the NL East title, but whose batting average was 106 points lower than Pujols' average. Pujols' average never dropped below .341 after April 9.

In the end, the voters decided that was too significant a difference to reward Howard's other advantages. Pujols won his second MVP award, the first time a Dominican-born player had won the award more than once. He also became the only Cardinal other than Stan Musial to win more than one MVP award.

"It's almost like a little boy getting a toy," Pujols said. "You're so excited waiting for that Christmas and to find out what you got. I knew I had a pretty good chance. I cried like a little boy, like I did in 2005."

Pujols received 18 first-place votes to 12 for Howard.

"You look at what he means to our team," said general manger John Mozeliak. "His consistency is one thing in itself. But his growth as a leader on this team has grown so much as well. Guys see how Albert is never satisfied with what he's done before. He's always trying to make himself better. That goes beyond numbers."

While the MVP award recognized Pujols' performance on the field, he also was rewarded after the 2008 season for his work off the field, being chosen as the recipient of the 2008 Roberto Clemente Award for contributions to the game, both on and off the field.

"I feel that's my responsibility," Pujols said, "whether it's in St. Louis or the United States or back in the Dominican Republic. At the end of the day, it doesn't matter what you did on the field, it's what you did off the field and lives you touched off the field.

"This is pretty special to me...not just because Roberto Clemente was Latin, but the lives that he touched and the legacy he left behind for us to follow: glorify God first and don't forget where we came from."

Both the MVP and Clemente awards came at a time when baseball was searching for someone to lead the game out of the "steroid era," and to restore fans' trust that not all players were guilty of using performance-enhancing drugs. Pujols was more than happy to step to the front as "the face of baseball" because, he said, he was not doing anything differently now than he had ever done.

"I have had a responsibility since I stepped into the big leagues, even before I put up the big numbers," Pujols said. "First of all I have a responsibility to represent God, which is who I play for, and my family and millions of fans in St. Louis, and that means on and off the field. I didn't have to wait eight years as a professional to deal with that responsibility. I'm a big believer that God won't give you anything you aren't capable of handling. If I am going to be in this position, he knows I can handle it.

"I can fool you guys (reporters) a lot, but I can't fool God. I've said this before and I mean it, I am a big believer that anything you do in the dark is going to come out in the light, and I fear God too much to do anything to disappoint him...I understand that we are living in a dark cloud right now, and that's pretty sad because I grew up

Pujols slides safely into third base well ahead of a Diamondbacks throw. Despite a slow start to his 2007 season, Pujols managed to pick up the pace in the second half.

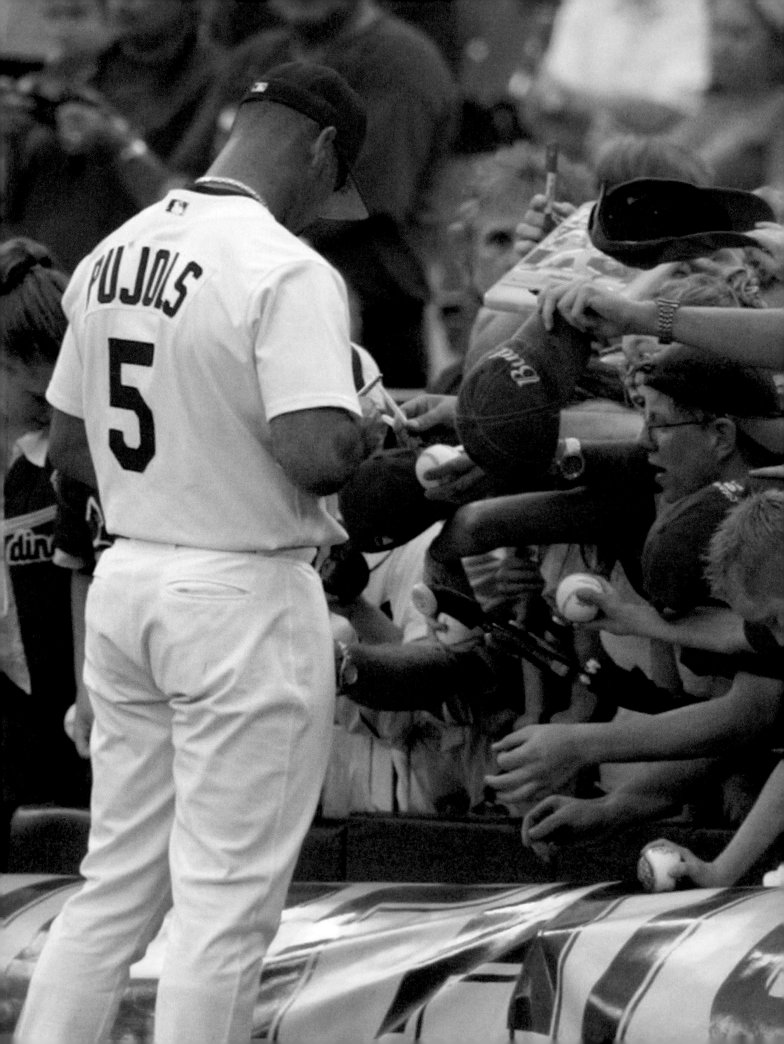

Ever popular with the St. Louis faithful, Pujols signs autographs just minutes before a game. His results on the field have been immeasurable, though his offensive stats through 2009 compare favorably with the great Joe DiMaggio at the same point in their careers.

loving this game and I still do."

A new generation of fans has also fallen in love with baseball because of Pujols, who will end the 2009 season as only the second player in National League history to lead the league in all three Triple Crown categories for a decade. He entered the 2009 season with a combined .334 average (eight points ahead of Colorado's Todd Helton), 319 home runs (41 more than Washington's Adam Dunn), and 977 RBIs (98 more than Lance Berkman of Houston).

The only other player to win the Triple Crown for a decade in the National League was Rogers Hornsby.

There is a reason his manager for every game he has ever played in the majors, La Russa, calls him "the perfect player."

"I've had guys I consider perfect pros, Carney Lansford in Oakland and Mike Matheny here," La Russa said. "But Albert adds in the complete player part of it. He is a perfect teammate and a perfect pro on and off the field. Albert plays the game exactly right in everything he tries to do.

"I get the opportunity to see everything about Albert. I get to see how he is with his teammates, how hard he pulls for them, how he is in the community. I see everything. I don't have that opportunity with other players."

The Sporting News put together a group of 150 people in the game—a blue-ribbon panel that included 13 Hall of Famers, 13 Cy Young winners, and 12 league MVPs—in early 2009 and asked them to select the top 50 players in baseball: Pujols received 55 first-place votes. The Yankees' Alex Rodriguez was a distant second.

Sports Illustrated asked 20 general managers and scouts which five players they would pick to start a franchise. Pujols received nine first-place votes and easily topped Tampa Bay's Evan Longoria in the overall balloting.

Pujols' coronation party as the best player in baseball came at the 2009 All-Star Game, played in his town of St.

(opposite) Called "the perfect player" by his manager, Tony La Russa, Pujols has proved time and time again that the statement is much more than mere hyperbole. If he can continue to rebound from injuries as well as he has, the Hall of Fame is a virtual certainty. (above) Pujols has earned the respect of his fellow major leaguers, baseball executives, and Hall of Famers, who rate him as the best player in the game today.

Louis. Every player in both leagues acknowledged it was Pujols' party. He arrived at the game leading the majors in homers (32) and RBIs (87), while hitting .332, the fourth-best average in the NL and 17 percentage points behind the Marlins' Hanley Ramirez.

He had arguably the best month of his career in June 2009, when he hit 14 homers, tying his career high for a month, and drove in a career-best 35 runs. He also hit .320 in the month, and 24 of his 31 hits went for extra bases.

"The fear he puts in pitchers speaks for itself," said the Phillies' Chase Utley. "He's just head and shoulders above everybody else right now."

Added Florida pitcher Josh Johnson, "Every time I turn on the TV, he's hitting a home run or driving somebody in."

Kansas City pitcher Brian Bannister said, "When he gets in the batter's box, if you pray, you start praying. And if you don t pray, you think about starting."

Opposing managers had no hesitation in discussing what it is like trying to figure out a way to attack Pujols.

"I don't think he has any holes to pitch to," said the Dodgers' Joe Torre. "That's frightening. The frightening part isn't getting him out, it's getting everybody around him out so that he doesn't hurt you too bad."

One manager who has faced Pujols perhaps more than any manager is Dusty Baker, first with the Giants, then with the Cubs, and now with the Reds. He also played with or against some of the greatest hitters the game has known, including Hank Aaron, Willie Mays, and Frank Robinson. He admits he is an unabashed Pujols' admirer.

"I hate to compare degrees of greatness. Great is great, whatever era you are in," Baker said. "Albert could

hit in any era. He's a big man with a wide stance, but he has a short compact stroke. Most people who stand that wide are not able to get around on pitches.

"He must study because he has an idea every time he goes up there what the pitcher is going to do to him and what he wants to do to the pitcher. There is no one way to pitch to him because he adjusts. And he adjusts rather quickly. He doesn't miss mistakes, and he hits good pitchers. Aaron, Griffey, Bonds, Mays, Musial, Williams...the great players...they don't pop up or foul off pitches they are supposed to hit hard in fair territory. That's the major difference.

"Some guys can get into a zone where they hit really well for several days in a row, or even a week or two, but the great ones are in that zone all the time. They have the ability to slow the game down, to slow the ball down. That ball must look like it stops in midair sometimes to Albert.

"The common denominator among all the great hitters has to be vision, the ability to pick up the ball. They must see things earlier than anybody else. Their vision has to be unparalleled."

Pujols' vision is very clear. He is focused on the future, and he is not concerned with how many career home runs he hits, or how many batting titles he wins, or if he ever wins the Triple Crown. He has a higher goal in mind.

"You know how I want people to remember me?" he asked. "I don't want to be remembered as the best baseball player ever. I want to be remembered as a great guy who loved the Lord, loved to serve the community, and who gave back. That's the guy I want to be remembered as when I am done wearing the uniform. That's from the bottom of my heart." ∎

With the Triple Crown in sight, Pujols charged hard into the 2009 All-Star break, dominating the majors in many offensive categories. The All-Star festivities in St. Louis served as a personal party for Pujols, who enjoyed the spotlight in his adopted hometown.